Braco and His Silent Gaze

Braco and His
Silent Gaze

Matthias Kamp, MD

BOOKS

Winchester, UK
Washington, USA

JOHN HUNT PUBLISHING

First published by O-Books, 2023
O-Books is an imprint of John Hunt Publishing Ltd., 3 East St., Alresford,
Hampshire SO24 9EE, UK
office@jhpbooks.com
www.johnhuntpublishing.com
www.o-books.com

For distributor details and how to order please visit the 'Ordering' section on our website.

ISBN: 978 1 80341 247 4
978 1 80341 248 1 (ebook)
Library of Congress Control Number: 2022937879

A CIP catalogue record for this book is available from the British Library.

Design: Lapiz Digital Services

UK: Printed and bound by CPI Group (UK) Ltd, Croydon, CR0 4YY
Printed in North America by CPI GPS partners

The author of this book does not dispense medical advice or
prescribe the use of any technique as a form of treatment for
physical, emotional, or medical problems without the advice of a
physician, either directly or indirectly. The intent of the author
is only to offer information of a general nature to help you in
your quest for emotional and spiritual well-being. In the event
you use any of the information in this book for yourself, which is
your constitutional right, the author and the publisher assume no
responsibility for your actions.

We operate a distinctive and ethical publishing philosophy in
all areas of our business, from our global network of authors to
production and worldwide distribution.

Contents

The interesting thing about Braco is that he can bring about changes in people...We always ask ourselves whether there's something there that science hasn't yet discovered, a kind of energy that can touch people.[1]

Professor Vladimir Gruden, MD, PhD

Preface

It's astonishing to stand in front of someone who does nothing but gaze in silence at the people attending his events. No inspiring talk, no new teachings or pearls of wisdom, above all no new religion—just silence. Braco gazes for a few minutes at the visitors standing in front of him—usually in groups of 100–150 people, but sometimes even more than 1000—and does not speak a word. Before his appearance, there is a short introduction for the visitors. Then, one group after another comes into the hall during the event. His appearance is usually accompanied by a short piece of music, or it is entirely silent. Forsaking any special gestures and simply dressed, the slim, medium-sized man with shoulder-length hair stands on a platform so that even the people in the back rows can see him. Seeing in this case means being able to look into his eyes. During the few minutes Braco stands in front of a group, his eyes traverse serenely across the rows. Some visitors are there for the sake of novelty; others are desperately hoping for a miracle; still others wear expressions of deep gratitude. Everyone seeks eye contact with the 53-year-old from Zagreb. The five to seven minutes are unlike anything else. Not a word is spoken—just silence and a gaze. But in this stillness, in the spiritual connection between the hundreds of pairs of eyes that seek Braco's gaze, something emerges that is beyond the grasp of the external senses. Every last corner of the room seems to be filled with something invisible that appears to the critical reason as mere nothingness, but that brings the open-hearted to tears. In an age otherwise known for many words and unending discussion, what's going on here?

These days, aren't the people who really matter those who can bring others onto their side with slogans, fiery speeches or clever words? But here stands a person, lacking all suggestive gesticulation, who apparently has no need to convince others by using words. He has the courage to stand before thousands of people in full awareness of his gift. Some scientists say that he has a gift the world has never previously seen in this form. Many of those in attendance, weary of the many words of our time, gratefully accept his silence. Who is this person who can simply take the stage for a few minutes, at prestigious conferences of experts, high-powered expos, or simple events in so many countries around the world, without doing or saying anything? Braco comes on stage, gazes at the groups of people for a few minutes and then leaves. The crowd of visitors does not consist purely of believers waiting in awe. Mostly it's people who are looking for a path in life, people who are despairing, or searching for peace and happiness or some higher purpose, who find their way to these events with Braco. Often they've already taken various paths, tried out different things, attended seminars and listened to the collected wisdom of multiple teachers. And yet this has manifestly not filled the void in their souls or answered their many questions about life. They're now looking for these answers from someone who says nothing, who hasn't spoken in public since 2004. His answer is silence and a gaze that lasts a few minutes. The effect is visible. You only have to look at the visitors who leave the room after encountering Braco's gaze: many have smiles on their faces and a sparkle in their eyes, and the relief in their souls and hearts is so palpable that my interest in Braco's work grew with each event. What is it that this man from Zagreb has been giving people through his eyes for more than 25 years? What can be so powerful that it only takes a gaze to transform other people internally and improve their lives? Who is Braco? What is the aim of his work?

Chapter 1

A Wordless Encounter

Braco, Zagreb, 2009

An Unexpected Gift

Braco is a human being like the rest of us. What makes him different from us is his gift of helping people improve their lives through his silent gaze. According to the statements of a large number of people, through his gaze something special that cannot be seen or heard, but that can certainly be felt, is present in the room. These people are convinced that the miracles, both great and small, that they experience through their encounter with Braco's gaze are the consequences of an invisible force or energy that works through his gaze and has the power to help them. But what do you need to do to be able to accept this person's unforeseen gift? At live events with Braco, visitors report on their experiences and in this way bring what happens invisibly more clearly into view.

> A strong sense of peace and serenity filled me, including on an emotional and mental level. All my wearying thoughts and worries ceased. I really found peace. I also saw how other people around me, like my elderly mother, all found peace in Braco's vicinity and how they came to terms with life's challenges in a completely new and different way. It's a big deal for me and for all the others. I feel very grateful. It's an occasion where you're connected with life and you just feel thankful simply to be allowed to be here. It's tremendous.[2] (Woman at an event in Croatia)

During those few minutes as Braco stands in front of the crowd, many of those in attendance gradually awaken to the perception that he is sharing something very real with them through his gaze. It's something invisible, something that's both alien and familiar at the same time. Florian, a young man from Austria, put it in the following words:

> There's something in his gaze that touches me on a deep level, a level that I otherwise can't access. In these moments, I feel connected with myself.[3]

As I heard again and again in conversations, the energy in Braco's gaze can illuminate a person's inner life. (The term "energy" is not entirely accurate, but I will use the word for the sake of simplicity.) Without wise or clever words, promoting no new teaching or philosophy, amid the enveloping stillness, a process of self-discovery is evidently set in motion. For many, it's a completely new experience. Braco wisely decided in 2004 to cease speaking in public. In an age of many words and endless discussion, a time of countless lies and information overload, many people find it comforting to encounter someone who has the courage to remain silent.

The Encounter

Trusting in his gift, Braco appears before groups of people and gazes at them for a few minutes in silence. His clothing is unremarkable. In clear awareness of his gift, he radiates unpretentious simplicity and humility. Yet he doesn't engage in any kind of spiritual or meditative practice. Based on my observation, he doesn't prepare himself in any particular way for the encounters with his gaze. It is a pure gift. He is simply there, making himself available for something that is greater than him and working through him. I could feel it as an invisible presence that was so directly there that you felt you could grasp it with your hands. I saw numerous stunned expressions on the faces of people who, through Braco's gaze, felt touched by something that so thoroughly surpassed their notions of beauty and grandeur that they could no longer find words for it. Below I will present without comment some statements that I heard at events with Braco. Some of the visitors had already been to an event several times. Others were coming for the first time, often following the recommendation of friends, and in most cases without any prior knowledge of Braco:

It's just an indescribable feeling. You can't explain it. You have to feel it for yourself.[4]

I've never felt anything like it in my entire life.[4]

I'm a completely different person. Before this, I couldn't even imagine such beauty in life.[4]

I've never felt such powerful positive energy in any other person.[4]

I honestly have to say that it works and I would never have imagined that energies like that really are there.[4]

You can't describe it. It's such a feeling of happiness and, how can I put it, something so wonderful. Contentedness.[4]

I came without any expectations. A friend told me about it. I noticed it's just crazy how much good it does you. You're so joyful. You have positive energy. It's like a light turning on inside you.[4]

As the writings and teachings of many traditions from East and West have long reminded us, we are far more than our external senses can grasp. Yet the rationalist insights of our times point in a different direction, to the point of seeing human beings only as biological machines. In this view, a higher spiritual dimension is an illusion. Those who persist in holding this view of human beings will find it difficult to access whatever it is that helps people through Braco. It is said that every tree is known by its fruits. The fact that Braco has been appearing before thousands of people for more than two decades and helping them in his own particular way speaks for itself. I've met multiple people who have gone to his events again and again for years or decades out of gratitude for the help they've received. There's also a remarkably large number of testimonials from people from all walks of life. Evidently a visitor's cultural background or religion is unimportant. Most of those I talked to spoke in similar terms of positive changes in their lives—just from a few minutes of being part of a group looking into Braco's eyes.

Ultimately, some critically minded person will always discover something to find fault with and will look for ways to argue that it's impossible to convey real help of this type and extent just through eye contact. There are also many concepts and categories that can be used to force an inexplicable phenomenon like Braco's gaze to fit into pre-existing definitions. Through my profession and many personal experiences, I'm familiar with these objections and arguments. I can understand someone who argues like this and expresses his or her lack of understanding. But I believe that in this time of change, it's better to respect phenomena that are far beyond our everyday experience.

This book is not intended to provide medical evidence of Braco's gift. Braco doesn't try to convince any of his audience members with rhetoric, or fascinate them with his wisdom. Even in private conversations with him outside the events, this doesn't happen. In stillness and in his own way, he makes something available that you are free to accept or reject. This something becomes reality for every visitor who perceives concrete changes to and within themselves. The "proof" thus remains a very personal matter.

There's no need for any special preparation for the encounter with Braco and his gaze. It's enough just to look Braco in the eyes during an event. This can be done online free of charge through live streaming (www.braco-tv.me) or at in-person events in various cities around the world. It's helpful to be quiet, though. There is external stillness when we go to a quiet place, but internal stillness is even more valuable. Many attendees experience something in Braco's gaze that simply quiets their unease. Without personal effort, inner peace enters in.

Braco Is Not a Healer

In terms of reason and logic, and our previous conceptions of life, what happens around Braco and his silent gaze will remain incomprehensible, because for the external senses nothing happens. Understandably, it's difficult for some people to comprehend that this external nothingness without words or visible activity can be the medium for something else. Perhaps it requires precisely the absolute simplicity of this silent gaze to convey what has helped so many people in today's world through the eyes of Braco. The Swiss professor Alex Schneider, a physicist, and founder and director of one of the world's largest conferences on healing and paranormal science, puts it in the following words:

> At the beginning of many path-breaking phenomena, there is skepticism, alienation, fear and often rejection. Our minds, for all their intellectual training, are not always sufficient to truly grasp the unknown...Braco has a striking effect on people's consciousness without any accompanying theories, philosophies or teachings. Born with corresponding charisma, he has the effect of a "normal," congenial and endearing person simply through his wordless presence. Most people who come to his meetings immerse themselves in this atmosphere and feel a transformation in themselves without having to interpret it. They gratefully accept the effects: a fuller sense of life or healing for body and soul.[5]

The notion of classifying Braco as a healer may seem convincing, but it's not correct. Braco doesn't know the vast majority of those who come to his events, and certainly isn't aware of their afflictions. During a meeting, the only contact between him and participants, who always come to him in groups, consists of a few silent minutes in which he stands before hundreds of people and looks at them. He doesn't concentrate on solving any particular health problem and is outwardly passive during the few minutes of his gaze. He has no personal influence on what happens there. His family and friends come to his events just like all other attendees because, as he told me, he cannot deliberately influence the effect of his gaze. Aid or improvement can never be promised. The goal of his special manner of working is to improve people's lives through his gift.

Even so, Braco respects the medical profession and the work of physicians. He doesn't see his activity as an alternative to medical treatment. Treatment remains in the hands of doctors and therapists. Those who come to his events should continue medical treatment and supervision even after attending. Braco would consult a doctor for himself and his family and heed the doctor's advice. His work has nothing in common with any typical medical or healing activity. He doesn't eliminate illness through his work. Instead, what lies in his gaze awakens something in people that can bring about improvements in the most diverse areas of life. In the words of Professor Schneider:

> Braco...repeatedly insists that he isn't a healer. He doesn't go to people to fight a particular malady. He seeks to reach them in a very deep, mostly unconscious part of themselves. If this is stimulated, harmonized, brought more into consciousness, then physical, mental and social disorders disappear. With Braco, the healing process is therefore of an entirely atypical kind, and if all factors fit together, it is much more effective and longer lasting than many other therapies, even more so than the spiritual healing we are familiar with.[6]

Professor Schneider invited Braco to his international conference in Basel in 2006 and then wrote a book about him in which he tried to explain the Braco phenomenon using his decades of experience as a trained physicist and respected consciousness researcher (Prof. Alex Schneider, *Braco: Die faszinierende Welt von Mythos und Wissenschaft* [English: *Braco: The Fascinating World of Myth and Science*]). Other scientists have also sought an explanation of what it is that brings about improvements in people's lives through Braco's gaze. Some speak of energy, information, or consciousness as the cause of the changes in the lives of those in attendance. There are neat theories that describe particular aspects of the phenomenon, but there is no satisfactory explanation. For those who come to events with Braco, their personal experience is proof of the reality of Braco's gift. Their reports are helpful for outsiders who find it difficult to imagine that a simple gaze might offer relief. Some say it's the power of unconditional love that brings about the miracles effected through Braco's gaze.

Awakening the Inner Life of People—the Most Important Task of Our Time

Whether our thoughts are pleasant or unpleasant, they become reality. However, they do not become reality by chance. Instead, we plan and develop them with a lot of effort in the unconscious part of our personality. Ultimately, we are what we think, and let us also add that we are what we feel. Our mental world becomes reality.[7]
Professor Vladimir Gruden, MD, PhD

Visitors from multiple European cities report on their feelings after they encounter Braco's gaze:

You can't describe that moment. There's a certain relief and also something inexpressible as well. I think it's ungraspable.[8]

I don't know. Something strange, something fantastic.[8]

I felt like I never had before—beautiful and somehow more powerful...[8]

It's a very intense light that he awakens in people...[8]

I can't explain it. If I could explain it, it wouldn't be so wonderful.[8]

When he looked at me, I felt like someone was wiping away all my worries.[8]

In this book, I've included a number of reports that describe changes in the physical, mental or social spheres as they were experienced by those attending Braco's events, and also changes in the consciousness of attendees. When it comes to physical and psychological improvements, I am restricting myself to simple, clearly comprehensible processes. The full spectrum of help and health improvements that come about through Braco's gaze is far broader.

As mentioned above, such an unusual phenomenon as Braco and his silent gaze is a challenge for our modern times. His gift cannot be adequately explained rationally and intellectually. But there are many people who have experienced a change or improvement in their lives after encountering Braco and his silent gaze. It's not for nothing that thousands come to Zagreb in November each year, bringing flowers for his birthday, to express their gratitude. On the other hand, there are also people who have no idea what to make of Braco and his gift. Still others experience changes but do not attribute much meaning to them for their own life. Braco does not seek disciples. He does not want to form groups. He is not a guru or a spiritual leader. He only travels to different cities and countries when invited. He comes, gazes and leaves. As already mentioned, what each person makes of this experience remains a very personal matter.

The physician and professor Vladimir Gruden of Zagreb speaks of the "unknown" that Braco gives through his gaze. It has no name, is invisible to the rational mind, and cannot be captured in thoughts and words, but is accessible to feelings. Professor Gruden avoids using a familiar term for this. The "unknown" is not something mysterious for him. It's a part of life, but it's unfamiliar to many people in our time. Apparently, what works through Braco's gaze has a particular quality for the inner life of a great number of people. The changes, often accompanied by strong feelings of happiness and peace, can also be an expression of an inner awakening. "Becoming bright inside," a feeling of being charged and animated from within, is a very real experience for many visitors. According to Professor Gruden, Braco is able to restore people's connections to their true selves.

For some visitors to the events, the internal changes are also associated with improvements in various areas of their lives. This leads to improvements in life in the psychological, physical and even social dimensions. But I will go into this in more detail later with examples. Perhaps something in Braco's gaze reaches a level in people that has previously been little known but is decisive for our lives. Life is much grander, more beautiful and more complex than everyday life would suggest. Perhaps modern people live only on the surface of what life really is, like a wave in the ocean. All traditions point unmistakably to people's inner being as the place where the key to freedom for each individual lies. Our modern times do not need an optimization of existing concepts, but a new image of human beings that puts people's consciousness and inner lives first. The breathtaking technological developments of the last 200 years have made us forget our inner grandeur. The unknown inner life and its powers are often mystified out of ignorance. But a person's soul is just as much a part of natural life as their body. Many scientists who have taken a closer look at Braco see in him the visible expression of what humankind needs most today. His coming at a time of change and disorientation apparently has special meaning. Among the multitude of spiritual teachers who want to enlighten people about their true origins and inner life in lectures and seminars, Braco stands out as special with his silent gaze. William Tiller, an American consciousness researcher and Stanford emeritus professor, sees Braco as the leading figure of the new paradigm.

If you believe the scientists who have engaged in exploring consciousness and the soul, the meaning of each person's spiritual life goes far beyond their personal life. These days, the assumption is that all people are connected at a certain level of their consciousness. So we human beings are individuals, and at the same time, on one level of our consciousness, we are one. Our personal lives affect the whole, and the whole affects our personal lives. We repeatedly hear from different traditions that people carry great treasures in their souls, a spark of the great light, a part of the source of all being, and for some, a part of the creator, God. This gives human life a meaning that is simply inconceivable. We have mostly forgotten ourselves and the unheard-of possibilities that are hidden in our souls. This can also be seen in the catastrophic quality of life experienced by many people today, especially the elderly. Our modern lifestyle, generally, does not give people a sense of purpose that can still sustain them in old age. The usual course of a person's life lacks all signs of a higher commission or purpose for that life. Some find this in the practice of a religion or various philosophies.

I believe that the people of our time are at a crossroads as to whether or not to embrace the true grandeur of their lives. But it's not enough to read or hear about it or to discuss it. This grandeur can only be experienced and felt. The awakening of people's inner lives is the most important task of our time. Just as a plant needs sunlight, water and fertilizer, so the human soul needs energy, stillness and attention to be able to grow. It is the stillness and the energy in Braco's gaze that bring about changes in the inner life of the people who seek him out. These changes lead to the attention of many being again directed inward. For a great number of people, the way back to oneself would not be possible without help. The mental and emotional entanglements with external and internal aspects of our life are too strong. Our power-sapping, dissipated way of life has robbed most people of the spiritual energy needed to take the path inward despite all obstacles. Through his gift, Braco offers a simple but effective opportunity for everyone to find their true selves again and thus happiness and meaning as well.

All the Pain Disappeared

Conversations with visitors at Braco's events are very helpful for getting a deeper insight into the phenomena surrounding him. The reports of long-standing complaints being improved or completely resolved in a short time, and thus in clear connection with a visit to an event with Braco, were particularly impressive for me.

In Berlin, Germany, I spoke to a 55-year-old woman who enthusiastically reported how her life had improved because of Braco. Since 2007 she had been suffering from increasing pain in her right shoulder, which she said had been traced to chronic inflammation and calcification in the shoulder area. Due to the pain, she could only move her arm to a limited extent and was unable to carry anything. The discomfort grew worse over the years. Eventually, even slight movement caused severe pain in the right shoulder. An MRI (magnetic resonance imaging) examination was followed by an initial surgical procedure, then more surgery the same year. Both operations failed to bring the desired relief, and she also fell on the affected shoulder. Regular physiotherapy and rehabilitation brought only slight improvement. A friend told her about Braco, and at the end of 2012 she attended an event in Berlin. Skeptical of any chance of success, she only went to please her friend. Here is an excerpt from her report:

> During the encounter with Braco's gaze, it was like I was liberated and I felt great relief. Tears were running down my face, which I couldn't explain at all. For the next two days, I had much more severe pain in my right arm. And after those two days, I could suddenly move my arm freely. After five

years, I'm now pain free. I can pick up my grandson again, move my arm in any direction, and do the housework by myself. I ride a bike and I'm mobile again.[9]

In addition, as a result of a mental trauma 20 years earlier, this woman suffered from a compulsion to inflict pain on herself. After giving birth to her son, her uterus had to be removed. Since then, she didn't truly feel like a woman. In order to endure this emotional pain, she would deliberately harm herself on her arms and legs with sharp stones or a razor blade. The physical pain brought mental relief. But instead of getting better, the episodes of self-harm increased over the years. For the last two years, she had harmed herself several times each week. She was given a diagnosis of borderline personality disorder. During all those years, her condition was resistant to therapy. She went to psychologists and psychiatrists and also sought help in clinics. It's well known that such mental disorders are very difficult to treat. Since her encounter with Braco, the episodes of self-harm no longer occur:

I had my most recent episode of self-harm a few days before the first encounter with Braco. The wounds hadn't yet healed. But since the encounter in fall 2012, I've never felt the need again. It doesn't reoccur even in personally stressful situations. It's never been like this in the last 20 years.[9]

In Amsterdam, I met Jose after an event. He had suffered serious heart attacks at the age of 39 and 62. Despite bypass surgery and frequent examinations by cardiac catheter and placement of stents, the medical tests found that his heart had limited capacity and reduced cardiac ejection (EF) (2013 cardio MRI, EF left ventricle: 28%). He had to give up working. He said that he couldn't walk more than a hundred meters before he reached his limit. He loved cycling, but it was no longer possible. Here is Jose in his own words:

My wife started looking for spiritual things on the Internet. At some point she found Braco's website. We went for the first time in October 2014. At first it didn't mean anything to me, but something attracted me to it, so I went again. The third time, I felt a warm feeling surrounding my heart. Between the third and fourth time, my symptoms improved significantly. I can now ride a bicycle for 30 kilometers and walk for 45 minutes without a pause. I feel good and healthy.[10]

I spoke to Eugenia, a medical assistant, in Munich. For three years she had been suffering from increasing pain in her right knee. Whether she was standing or walking, there was always pain. Cycling was especially bad. An MRI scan revealed a meniscus tear and cartilage damage, which was traced to an injury from dancing. Even cortisone injections by an orthopedic surgeon didn't help. She enthusiastically told me that after attending an event with Braco, she no longer had any pain. She is now able to stand for an extended time and can walk as long and as quickly as she wants. Cycling, even for many kilometers, is again possible without any discomfort.[11]

The books of Drago Plečko, a well-known Croatian scientist who has investigated Braco and his work for years, also report remarkable improvements in chronic diseases among those who attend Braco's events. For example, he describes spontaneous relief from severe fecal incontinence (inability to retain stool) in a woman from Munich. A young woman suffering from anorexia was brought to an event by her parents and soon recovered. A man with epilepsy found that the number of his seizures decreased significantly. Improvements in rheumatoid arthritis, cancer, chronic pain, diabetes mellitus, various allergies, bronchial asthma, depression and much more are described.

I clearly remember an event with Braco in Memmingen, Germany, in 2019. Shortly before the beginning of the session, I met a woman who told me how the edema (water retention) in her legs that she had long suffered from had disappeared after attending several events with Braco.[12] Later I was approached by an elderly man whose joint pain, which his doctor had traced to osteoarthritis (wear and tear), had simply disappeared after his first encounter with Braco and his gaze.[12] Annette, a colleague of mine, reported at an event in Munich that ever since she started attending Braco's events, she no longer had high blood pressure, although she still faced stress at work.[12] A woman in Munich in her early forties told me that she had suffered from endometriosis (a condition causing severe inflammation and abdominal pain in women and heavy menstrual bleeding) for over eight years. Hormone therapy and surgery had not helped. She also had a fibroid 3 centimeters in diameter in her uterus and had been plagued by anxiety for years. After attending an event with Braco in Munich, all the pain was gone, the menstrual bleeding was normal, she was no longer anxious, and a short time later, her gynecologist could no longer find signs of a fibroid.[12]

Ivanka, with whom I spoke in Berlin, suffered from a serious chronic pain disorder, muscular rheumatism, also known as fibromyalgia. The pain was constant and was only somewhat alleviated by treatment. She was forced to take early retirement. In all those decades, she was never able to be free of symptoms despite all the treatments in clinics and from specialized doctors. In the presence of Braco's gaze at an event in Berlin, she felt a tingling sensation throughout her body, heaviness in her legs, and then a feeling of happiness. She left the room free of pain. That was 14 years ago. Her astonished doctor has confirmed in writing that she is free from the chronic illness.[13]

During a visit to Europe, Julio from Mexico told of an extraordinary improvement in his condition: ankylosing spondylitis (a rheumatoid disease of the spine). Just by taking part in various sessions with Braco online via live streaming, the condition of his health improved from session to session, much to the astonishment of his doctors, with the symptoms regressing.[14]

Help with Life through a Gaze

Events such as those described above occur again and again, but they're not the rule. Some attendees feel nothing at the beginning or only a slight sense of calm, while others, as mentioned, find no words to express the depth of their experiences. Some people don't even consciously perceive the first signs of a change in themselves because they are too externally focused or don't know what to do with the internal precursors, such as a feeling of peace or joy. Again and again, changes appear in the hours and days after an event. The experiences are so individual that no rule can be formulated. The well-known neurologist and psychiatrist Professor Dr. (med.) Dumitru Dulcan conducted a small study with the participants after an event with Braco in Bucharest, Romania. He found that around 10% of the participants didn't feel anything, while 90% of those present were obviously undergoing a psychological or physical process and perceived changes in and within themselves:

> I conducted a study based on the experience reports of more than 1,500 participants, and consequently I am of the opinion that Braco in fact has an effect on the mind, the soul and the physical body.[15]

Rudina, a medical colleague of mine, told me about a similar experience:

> I asked some of my friends and also patients or even strangers to accompany me to an event with Braco or to watch a DVD about him. I was able to determine that in 99% of the cases, a feeling of calm, peace and wellbeing was the most common experience.[16]

Certainly an inner openness and a willingness to accept new things are important. But there are also examples of people who went to an event with Braco only at the urging of friends and with an attitude of cynicism and rejection, yet still experienced astonishing improvements in health.[17, 18] During the conversations, I also learned of changes in the social sphere, for example with personal relationships in the context of marriage, family and work, in proximity with attending an event with Braco. The fact that people repeatedly report improvements in the circumstances of their lives in connection with the online broadcast of Braco's gaze via live streaming also makes you take notice. At these online events, Braco gazes into the camera from his center in Zagreb, and visitors from all over the world can look into his eyes via the screen. There have been online events with Braco since 2010. People from more than 70 countries are currently participating in these free events.

Lorette had heard about Braco from a friend. She lives in Palestine and participated in an online event via live streaming. In her own words:

> At first I thought: "Is this really true?" So much has changed in my life after the live stream with Braco's gaze! A short time later, I found a new job and a house—something I had never dared dream of. My adult children and their families have also been helped. Everything started to change for the better, even if they didn't participate in the live stream event with Braco. During this time I felt an indescribable feeling of happiness, joy and deep peace.[19]

In another case, I learned of a skeptical husband who was struggling with his difficult relationship with his daughter. For five years, she had refused to see him, and she was also unreachable for him by phone. Then, at the urging of his wife, he watched two live streaming events with Braco online. A short time later, his daughter called him back for the first time. Since then, contact between them has been restored.[20] At an event in Böblingen near Stuttgart, a woman reported a similar incident:

> For 20 years, my former husband had no contact with my son. He had no desire for it. The silence lasted for a long time. I came here and wished with all my heart that this could be made right and that father and son would talk to each other again. After attending an event with Braco for the second time, my former husband, the father of my son, got in touch. After 20 years, he wanted to see his son again.[21]

Of course it can be difficult when people who attend events expect changes and think that everything has to happen immediately. Even in the area of spirituality, a "supermarket mentality" has developed with the expectation that inner progress or a desired improvement in living conditions should take place in a short time, as if you were grabbing something from the shelf and dropping it into a shopping cart. But the improvements in many spheres of life effected by Braco's gaze, which are inexplicable to our rational understanding, are also based on an orderly regularity. They certainly can't be influenced by a demanding attitude. We live in a time of transition that is characterized by changes in all areas of life. Much that seemed impossible or unthinkable years ago is now becoming possible. Perhaps in these times it's simply important to be open to something new that exceeds all our previous ideas. In Berlin, I met Elfi at an event. Her first meeting with Braco was online via live streaming. In her own words:

> I've been meditating for many years, but in all those years I've never felt such calm. All I did was look Braco in the eyes for a few minutes online on my PC.

Since this experience, a very uncomfortable herpetic genital itching she had suffered from for years has not recurred. She felt psychological relief, as if "a burden had been taken from her." Since then, her life has gone smoothly, and there have also been wonderful changes in her professional life.[22]

She Thought Only of Her Sister...

An extraordinary aspect of the effects of Braco's gaze involves improvements in the lives of people who are not personally present at an event. In these cases, participants request help for their friends and relatives by taking them to an event in the form of a photo or in their thoughts. In Esslingen, Germany, in spring 2019, I had a conversation with a woman in her forties from Reutlingen. In her own words:

> I can clearly remember how last year I was at an event with Braco here in Esslingen. I had a fervent desire to help my sister in Sydney. She had suffered from alcoholism for over ten years and couldn't get away from it. Just before Braco offered his gaze, I thought of her with a wish that she would find help. That was on a Saturday. A few days later I phoned my mother in Sydney, who told me that my sister had given up drinking that weekend. She had felt a strong sense of revulsion and had been avoiding alcohol ever since. That had never happened in the last ten years.[23]

Peter is from Australia. I met him in Zagreb in 2018 while he was vacationing in several European countries. He had learned of Braco in 2014 and went to an event in Sydney. His fervent wish was to find help for his 93-year-old mother. She had broken her hip and pelvis in a fall and was lying in the hospital in severe pain. She was very weak. The doctors treating her advised him to let her die, since the end appeared to be imminent. At the time, he took a photo of her to the event with Braco in Sydney, and asked for help. A few days later, he received a call from the hospital. They told him that his mother had unexpectedly recovered. She was able to walk 50 meters without pain, which hadn't been possible even before the fall. To the astonishment of the doctors and nurses, she was cheerful again and had resumed eating: a completely transformed woman. The trauma surgery head physician was unable to explain this series of events. When we met in Zagreb, Peter told his story with great excitement and also showed photos of his mother from before and after the event. They documented a striking change. His mother lived in good health for another seven years.[24]

Marina from Croatia brought a photo of her daughter to an event with Braco. Her daughter suffered from anxiety and chronic headaches. She didn't even dare to go to the toilet by herself. She also stuttered. Speech therapy was unable to help the child. According to Marina, the anxiety and stuttering disappeared after she attended an event with Braco's gaze just a few times, while holding a photo of her child.[25] A woman from Switzerland brought a photo of her sister to an event with Braco in Zurich. Not long after, her sister in Canada experienced a dramatic improvement in her health.[26] At an event in the USA on the west coast, a woman told of a special experience. Years earlier, she had taken a photo of her mother to a meeting with Braco. In her own words:

My mother has been an alcoholic for 50 years. I took a photo of her and kept it close to my heart when I first went to an event with Braco two years ago. That same weekend, my mother called my younger brother and asked him to throw out all the alcohol in her house. I called her yesterday and she said she has now been sober for two years.[27]

A visitor from Croatia reported:

I have been coming here to see Braco since last year because of my son. I had a lot of problems with him. He used hard drugs for more than eight years. After a month—I went to see Braco five times—it was over. He has totally changed, as if he's not the same boy I had before.[28]

The particular phenomenon of an effect across great distances represents a challenge for people of our time. It requires modern scientific views that acknowledge that people are connected to one another on a higher level of consciousness. In this state of consciousness, spatial distance is inconsequential. Someone in attendance can connect another person to the event through a photograph or in their thoughts. This is confirmed not only by the reports listed as examples above, but also by a number of others that I learned of. With a clear temporal connection, changes make themselves felt in people's lives just because someone close to them asked for help on their behalf. Professor Schneider, the Swiss researcher, writes in his previously mentioned book:

There are astonishing cases where healings, again in the broadest sense, take place in people who live far away via photographs that the participants carry with them. The reports of a participant experiencing an inexplicable improvement in their social environment are similarly startling. As already mentioned, one must not argue on the basis of inapplicable concepts, for example whether or not it's possible for a healing exchange of information like that to take place over a large distance. The concept of distance does not apply to this set of events between a participant and his sick friend in New York or the tense atmosphere at his place of work, which occur in a different state of consciousness. To put it entirely correctly: in this state of consciousness, the places are one.[29]

Just Watching a DVD Has a Particular Effect

Visitors to the events with Braco have told me that books and films about Braco convey more than just information. Some people draw strength for their everyday lives from reading a book or watching a DVD or film about Braco on YouTube (YouTube: Braco official channel). What has astonished me is that even in this way, concrete changes take place in people's lives. In Munich, I met Monika (aged 55) after an event with Braco. She explained how she had suffered from back pain for more than 40 years. Doctors had diagnosed her with vertebral displacement in the lower part of the lumbar spine (spondylolisthesis). As a child, she had often had to carry heavy loads. The pain got worse each year, and from the age of 14 onward she was in constant pain. Painkillers brought some relief, but an operation was ruled out due to the risk at that time. Chiropractic treatments brought short-term improvement. After years of this, she stopped treatment and just lived with the pain. Monika in her own words:

> In fall 2014 I visited my neighbor. She was watching a DVD when I entered her apartment. She wanted to turn it off, but I told her, "Just let it play," and I sat down next to her. As I sat and watched the DVD—it was about a man named Braco—I suddenly felt a tingling sensation all over my body. It was like a shiver. After about half an hour I got up and went back to my apartment. When I woke up the next morning, I found that for the first time in decades I could get out of bed in the morning without pain.[30]

Since then, Monika has remained free of pain. Sitting or standing for a long time no longer causes her difficulty, and she can also sleep without pain. In the morning she finds it easy to get out of bed.

Swiss professor Alex Schneider reported a similar experience. After watching a DVD of Braco, "vexing pain," as he called it, that had plagued him for days spontaneously disappeared.[31] A woman from Zagreb explained during an event how she had seen a Braco DVD at a friend's house. As she watched, she felt intense heat throughout her body:

> It was like a current running through my whole body. I stood up and couldn't believe it—I could walk without pain. That hadn't been possible for a long time. For years, I had problems with my back and feet. All the pain was gone from my body. I made the 20-minute walk home on foot and was amazed at the lack of pain. You wouldn't believe in something like that unless you've experienced it yourself. I immediately bought flowers for my friend out of gratitude for her telling me about Braco.[32]

It is futile to look for explanations. Monika had no prior knowledge and no hope of recovery. Over the decades, she had become accustomed to the pain. She watched the DVD in her neighbor's home by sheer accident. This also applies to the experience described by Professor Schneider. A friend had given him the DVD about Braco. He left it lying around for weeks before he watched it. He had no prior knowledge of Braco and his work. In the third case, too, it was more an interest aroused by her friend's encouragement that motivated the woman to watch the DVD. There was no prior knowledge in this case either.

Chapter 2

An Awakening in the Soul

There is no difference between the thought of an embrace and the embrace itself. When I become one with everyone standing before me for a fraction of a second, that is this embrace. Invisible, but impactful.[33]
Braco in conversation with Drago Plečko

Burdens and Darkness Give Way

In November 2019, I attended a large spirituality expo in Barcelona. It was Braco's first appearance in Spain. Among the reports of people in attendance, I vividly remember one young man. He said:

When I looked in Braco's eyes, I felt a darkness that had haunted me for years suddenly grow weaker and weaker. All its power was just taken away.[34]

This isn't an uncommon experience. In other countries, too, participants choose similar words to describe their inner experience while looking into the eyes of Braco. There is talk of a negativity or darkness that drains energy away from the soul. Many perceive a feeling of psychological relief and liberation in themselves, as if something heavy had been taken from them.

For more than 17 years, Veselina (aged 56) had suffered from depression. I met her in Berlin at an event with Braco. Her life was marked by sadness and dejection, which had intensified at the death of her husband. She hadn't visited a doctor because she didn't believe there was any help for her. A friend made her aware of Braco and challenged her to go to an event with him in Berlin. Here is Veselina in her own words:

I went along, but I was sad and all knotted up inside. When Braco came, I started crying. I couldn't hold back. A few days later, as I was lying on the couch, I felt like something was opening in the area of my solar plexus. It was like I started smiling from there. It was the first inner smile I'd had in many years. Since then I can smile again, and from the heart. I rediscovered the feeling of joy that I had missed for so many years. Now I can laugh again.[35]

A pain in the joint at the base of Veselina's left thumb that had persisted for more than ten years, which doctors attributed to osteoarthritis caused by excessive strain while working as a housekeeper, also disappeared. It was constant pain day and night, aggravated with every movement of her thumb. At night, she wore a splint. It was only with the aid of ibuprofen that she could still work to some extent. After the event with Braco, the pain disappeared and did not recur even during strenuous cleaning work. She hasn't needed ibuprofen ever since.

A woman from France reported:

I had sadness inside me for many years and I tried out different techniques to help me feel better. After I first saw Braco's gaze online via live streaming ten months ago, that began to change rapidly. So much of the sadness has disappeared and I'm optimistic again.[36]

A 26-year-old woman I met in Munich had suffered from anxiety and panic attacks for more than six years. She had been in psychotherapeutic treatment for years, but it hadn't led to any significant improvement. Visibly moved, she explained:

During the first contact with Braco at a live event, I experienced an intense and indescribable feeling and inner calm. I cried a lot during the encounter. Since that day, the anxiety and panic attacks have completely disappeared.[37]

A woman from Los Angeles suffered from depression for many years. She had meditated for years and applied the techniques of positive thinking, but without success. Here she describes an encounter with Braco:

> It's like heavenly energy coming in, and a feeling of beauty and calm and happiness sets in. I love being present with Braco because there's nothing like it in the whole world. I have the feeling that God is looking at me through his eyes and hugging me. I was depressed for many years. When I saw Braco for the first time, the depression suddenly disappeared. It happened without me having done anything myself.[38]

She brought photos of family members to the next event with Braco:

> The last time, I brought pictures. A short time later my sister called me. I had never heard a positive word from her mouth. She was different now, and so many wonderful things happened with my children after that.[38]

From a psychological point of view, through gazing with Braco evidently inner psychological conflicts resolve. From a philosophical or spiritual point of view, one can assume that there are forces in our lives, some constructive and some destructive, that have a direct effect on the soul. In various religions and traditions, these forces have been given a wide variety of names. Perhaps through Braco's gaze a power is at work that is able to rebuild people spiritually and eliminate or reduce negative influences. Professor Gruden, a Croatian psychiatrist and psychotherapist, also noticed the astonishing psychological changes among participants in events with Braco. He noted:

Something good from the outside drives out that bad [stuff] from the inside.[39]

One man described what operates through Braco's eyes as a "manifestation of the good."[40] Some visitors also said:

I suddenly had the feeling that I had been given a new life, a second chance.[40]

Obviously, with serious opening up over a period of time, some people also experience a change in personality. The participants I spoke with told me that they felt they had become different (and according to their perception, better), more loving, more patient people. I was also able to observe a new self-confidence and greater self-esteem emerge. Again and again I heard:

Braco's gaze gave me back my freedom.[40]

Professor Vladimir Gruden, MD, PhD, was the most famous psychotherapist and psychiatrist in Croatia. As previously mentioned, he studied Braco and his gift and its effects on people and their inner lives for years. In his books *Bracos Blick 1* and *Bracos Blick 2* (English: *Braco's Gaze 1* and *Braco's Gaze 2*), he goes into great detail on the effects of Braco's gaze on human consciousness and the psyche. He also writes about changes in the inner life of people:

The people who leave Braco are no longer the same as those who came. This strange, inexplicable change that enables a better existence is just as fascinating the first time as it is the twentieth time. Each encounter completes the change a little more.[41]

Our inner life goes through changes and takes on a new, unfamiliar dimension. In it we experience health, inner peace and a qualitatively better self with a high potential for happiness. We feel a connection because we are not alone, but connected to a multitude of previously unknown elements of existence.[42]

Thoughts

A feeling of peace established itself, an endless serenity. It's not something we're experiencing. It's who we are. The impression is so strong that I felt like God was caressing us. It spreads out so wide. It's who we are and not something we're experiencing. We are this energy.[43]

A woman attending an event with Braco in Portugal

It's above all the way we deal with our thoughts that poses significant problems for people today. We are exposed to a multitude of our own memories and conclusions we've drawn, and in most cases we don't know how to deal with them. Worries, fears and concerns continuously well up from within, and there is often a pessimistic attitude toward life. Few people are aware of the fact that it's in our own hands to choose our thoughts. We should only think of beautiful things and let pessimism slip away, or we should turn our backs on it, regardless of history. But in most cases there's not enough strength to successfully resist the overpowering influence of thoughts with negative content. In his books about Braco, Professor Gruden writes:

Our thoughts hypnotize us, and our feelings evolve according to our thoughts. A thought combined with a feeling triggers an action. We spend our lives with such negative thoughts, which are a serious and powerful factor in autosuggestion. Positive thoughts would have the same effect and the same intensity, but with reversed polarity.[44]

People need to develop the ability to protect themselves. How many times have we caught ourselves with superficial, negative thoughts buzzing around our heads! And as they take control step by step, they poison lives by inciting people to say and do things for which they will be ashamed afterwards. Only a few people are aware of the possible connections between their mental world and the difficulties in their lives. Many have invested much of their mental energy in things that were not worth it.

The inner struggle with negative thoughts and feelings, or the ability to just let them go since they are "only" thoughts and feelings, makes people stronger. You begin to consciously focus your thoughts on positive things and reject lies, envy and despair. There is no more important work than working on yourself. The best thing in a human heart is the pursuit of goodness. This pursuit fills us with such clarity and lightness inside! Being good is what brings people closer to their souls. But this isn't easy, because people have a dual character. Many of us love only ourselves and look down on others. We may be jealous of the accomplishments of others and indifferent to their sufferings. The ability to take delight in others' happiness is the characteristic of a person who is full of inner light. There is no real freedom without this quality.

The transformation of a person who wants to change his or her behavior, thoughts or feelings can be painful at the beginning. It's often not easy to change the path that you have taken for decades. But there are many beautiful inner experiences on the way to goodness that enable us to persevere and prevent us from falling back into our old patterns again and again. Sometimes, during that process of internal change, we feel pain in our soul. Everything that was previously clear and orderly is transformed into something pliable, wobbling and unclear. It seems as if your own inner world is collapsing. But if you make an effort and endure and overcome the painful effects, a window into the world of harmony will soon open. When the inner torment has been lived through, people gain a new perspective: clarity is restored, and it even exceeds the previous degree of clarity many times over.

Internal struggle, and thus also external struggle, is an unavoidable condition of life, but adversity of this kind can give us wisdom and a deeper understanding of life. Some say that life is a struggle, and that is why wars are fought and battles great and small are waged between people. The result of this contention is often death instead of life. But that is not the real meaning of conflict. It can be expressed in simple words that everyone who looks even somewhat consciously into his or her mental world can confirm: our real enemies are within us. That is the real meaning of conflict in life. Every day, every hour and every minute, this is where the conflict and struggle that decides our lives takes place. Negative feelings and thoughts emerge within us, and our challenge is to resist them internally. Then life becomes a struggle. It's easy to fall into the trap of these invisible "enemies" who reveal themselves to us as thoughts and feelings. How can we counter their constant influence? It is an inner act of strength, a personal struggle, which is very difficult when we have no solid footing inside us and do not know the true nature of this inner battle. A person's victory in his or her inner world is more valuable than winning a dispute, a battle or a war, because this victory brings life for the person individually and for everyone else as well.

Openness of the mind and personal fears can easily lead to disturbances in people's inner lives. We influence our fate through our thoughts and beliefs. But there are people who have developed the strength in themselves to ward off the negative mental influences that seek to dominate their inner lives. A person close to me, who has developed remarkable strength on the inner path, put it in the following simple words: "In short, my consciousness cannot come under such influence.

Everything that penetrates my consciousness is automatically corrected, so it has no effect." It is this corresponding filter inside which checks not only thoughts of the mind but also feelings, and thus prevents many unnecessary inner fights and tensions. Those who are aware of the seriousness of such negativity work on themselves so that this protection of their inner life can arise.

The constant interpretation of one's own thoughts and feelings and the behaviors and statements of others becomes a heavy burden for some people. It can cause aggression, fears and even delusions. Some people deal with these things for hours, days, weeks, months or even years. It can also lead to social withdrawal, avoidance of contact, and loneliness. The root cause: thoughts and feelings, products of fantasy and imagination that seem real and true and yet do not correspond to the truth. Some people need many decades, some their entire lives, to realize this, and many do not understand at all that the suffering in their lives was only because they believed in lies. I remember a simple old text whose exact source I do not know. But I would like to quote it here:

A certain man didn't know how to get rid of the troubles that plagued him. One day a wise man came to him and said: "Wake up and pray: 'God, free me from bad thoughts.'"

"Is that all?" the lonely and miserable man wondered.

"Yes, that's all," said the wise man.

The wretched man had nothing more to lose, so he started asking for this every morning, and soon things changed in his life. His bad thoughts left him and he became light and peaceful inside again. It was impossible to call him an unhappy man anymore because his real life had begun.

The bad thoughts had been given to this man to torment him. And the man didn't understand that by casting away these thoughts, he would also cast away the torment. His suffering wasn't over until he had realized this. He asked himself, "How could I have been so stupid?" But he needed his whole life to get wiser.

In most cases, parental upbringing, and preschool, elementary, secondary school and university education provide no knowledge about the nature of our mental world. So in people's everyday lives, it isn't perceived as separate from their own personal identity. Many still live according to Descartes' proposition: *Cogito ergo sum* (I think, therefore I am). This makes identifying yourself with your thoughts unavoidable. The lack of distance makes it difficult to recognize thoughts as something foreign to you and not as part of your own personal identity. In addition to the distorting effects of interpreting internal and external experiences, people's mental world is also governed by a false concept of time. Many live in the illusion of a mental past or future. The consequence of these habits is a multitude of "mental conversations." These conversations cause internal conflicts that shatter their peace of mind. Like an undercurrent, these negatively tinged thoughts and ideas suck the vitality from our hearts and paralyze our inner lives. They form an entryway into an invisible prison of our own construction, made of thoughts and feelings that are distilled into a multitude of continuously repeating stories.

Only a few people are aware of the game being played with them and realize that their thoughts are not part of their personal identity. These people discover that they are capable of observing their thoughts and feelings. But the observer cannot be identical to the thing being observed. As is heard more and more frequently in lectures and seminars these days, it is consciousness, one's own self, that perceives thoughts. Thoughts are therefore something alien, something outside of me. This realization is the basis for creating distance. In most cases, however, there is insufficient strength to climb out of the internal prison. In his book *Das Mysterium Braco 3* (English: *The Mystery of Braco 3*), Drago Plečko quotes from an interview with Braco. Plečko asked him what advice he would give people for their lives. Braco replied:

> Be good and do good. Be natural and just let it flow through you freely. Feel your body and observe your countless thoughts. Just let them be. Bad ones, good ones, ugly ones — just observe them. And now, as you read this, you should know that this is not meant symbolically, but literally. See your thoughts flowing through your mind and body, uninterrupted, free, supple…If you just leave them alone for a few seconds, you'll know exactly what I'm talking about.[45]

The gaze of Braco has a fundamental impact on the thought life of some people. Conversations with people attending his events showed me that their manner of thinking was changing in a positive direction. The contents of their inner lives were no longer a chaos of hope and despair. An encounter with Braco leads, as one visitor put it, to a "brightening within,"[46] which consequently appears again and again as a calming of agonizing thoughts, or even complete liberation from them. A "stillness in the soul" arises.[46] In the first few minutes of Braco's gaze, some visitors spontaneously perceive a feeling of inner liberation in connection with an extraordinary stillness in the soul.[46] This is felt as a release from a burden — "my chest is free again,"[46] "a new feeling of life is there"[46] — which brings tears to the eyes of many a person. There's also often talk of a completely new feeling of optimism that's unexpectedly perceptible and expresses itself as joy and feelings of happiness. The inner change is also connected with a feeling as if "the soul life is being lifted up to a higher level."[46] These are sensations that can last for a while in everyday life even after the encounter with Braco. A businesswoman from Zagreb who had suffered from the typical symptoms of burnout described her inner changes as if "her soul was vibrating on a higher frequency."[47] The symptoms of burnout completely disappeared after a few encounters with Braco's gaze. In some cases, what arises is the feeling of a previously unknown mastery of problems, difficulties in life, or inner psychological conflicts. Afterwards, visitors report that some of their problems have unexpectedly solved themselves or become less important, or that they have suddenly become aware of solution strategies. A good proportion of visitors feel confident that they can now cope more easily with the demands of life and approach things differently. At events in Germany, Croatia and Switzerland, visitors describe the experience of Braco's gaze:

When I come here, I feel like something is being taken from me. I'm full of energy, verve and strength. I'm coming because I just feel better.[48]

At first I was very skeptical, but now I'm convinced. When I got home after the event with Braco, I discovered that I was happier. It's like coming back to my childhood. The time when I was happy. And that's it.[48]

You feel like you're somehow connected to electricity. A powerful current of energy. When you come out, you feel like you're seeing everything with different eyes. As if you are getting a new level of energy. I don't know how to explain it logically. I don't know how to explain it scientifically, but help is being provided here.[48]

I felt the energy in the room before he was there. And the depth and the impact, it's very moving, very moving. What I feel now is relief.[48]

You can't really describe its impact on people. What he gives people is simply fantastic. It brings about something different in everyone. For me personally, it's just fabulous to live this feeling of freedom, to be open to life.[48]

The positive changes in people's inner lives lead them to turn their gaze inward. For many a visitor, these experiences are the beginning of a journey to oneself, a rediscovery of the life of one's own soul. Further down the line, a lasting change in a person's basic mood — toward optimism, affirmation of life, and joy — can also be observed again and again.

Silence

I had great expectations for finding out how silence can touch us in a world where there are so many words, always words, always, always. And that's what I wanted to experience. When Braco started, I didn't actually feel anything and I was sad. But a few moments later I felt something very interesting. I felt like a lead cloak was being pulled off me. Instead, I was wrapped in new clothing. I felt light, very light.[49]
Visitor at an event with Braco

Some people may have experienced silence while sitting outside late at night or early in the morning on vacation when there's no sound to be heard. But not all silence is the same. From the outside, the silence at an altitude of 2000 meters in the mountains can be just as quiet as in the valley, and yet there's something different about it. Silence doesn't just mean there's nothing there. It means that we aren't perceiving anything with our external senses. But this invisible content constitutes the difference between one silence and another. Perhaps you could put it like this: the silence at 2000 meters above sea level contains a different energy. Instead of energy, you could also simply say: it contains something different. Emotionally, it's perceived as being of higher value, without being able to define it more closely. Some people can feel these differences—that is, the different quality of silence between the two places. The well-known Bulgarian philosopher and educator Omraam Mikhaël Aïvanhov writes in his book *Der Weg der Stille* (English: *The Path of Silence*):

> Anyone who believes that silence reflects nothing but desert, emptiness or the absence of any activity, of any creation, or in a word, nothingness, is very mistaken.[50]

Aïvanhov speaks of a special silence in people that he has experienced in himself. He describes it as the silence of the higher self. One of the most famous of India's silent yogis, Ramana Maharshi, meditated for decades. To this day, Indians venerate him as a saint. In the Western world, he is considered one of the greatest sages of the twentieth century. Ramana Maharshi lived in silence. He rarely spoke. The all-pervasive and transforming power of silent teaching was his hallmark. For him, silence was his highest teaching. In it, he silently passed on what people need in order to find their true self again. His visitors usually sat in silence next to him to take in what he had to give.[51]

When Braco stands in front of the groups of people at the events, he is silent. But there's still his gaze. The silence that can arise inside us during the encounter with his gaze can bring with it great value for a person's inner life. It's a different kind of silence than in the places in nature described above. In the silence that can arise in an encounter with Braco's gaze, there's something very specific, which has the power to give a person the experience of inner liberation. As mentioned above, some visitors describe it as if they were being raised to a higher spiritual plane. Professor Alex Schneider, the Swiss researcher, speaks of a higher level of human existence to which people can be raised internally during the encounter with Braco. The silence that arises on this inner height is free of thought and all the mental ballast of the current situation in life. It's empty to our consciousness, but it carries a brightness in it. As one visitor put it, it's something that is "not of this world."[52] For many people, it's their first experience in life of an inner silence of this quality. People appreciate these inner changes as a personal gift of high value. This also applies to the other qualities that can be perceived in the inner silence. Professor Gruden:

> Silence is the most important witness of the truth. The truth is so real, so powerful and so infinite that silence is the only appropriate form of communication for it.[53]

More and more, stillness reveals itself in experience as our inner life's form of communication. It's like an emptiness in consciousness, a bowl containing space to accept something new. The new doesn't come from the familiar external world, but from the depths of your own soul. Some visitors experience an inexplicable optimism and joy without a cause. They also describe feelings of peace and serenity. Professor Gruden speaks of the unknown in the human soul becoming perceptible again in the stillness of the encounter with Braco's gaze. It's already been said several times that the path of truth lies in every person. To walk that path, we need stillness and vigilance to let the multitude of thoughts that seek to destroy the stillness pass by. Attentiveness lets us again hear the soft and tender voice in the stillness that has always spoken to us, the voice of our soul. What can we do when we don't know what to do? Professor Gruden summarizes in simple words:

> Be silent and look, be silent and act; that is to say: just keep living.[54]

> We should just remain calm, still, and wakeful, and every wish will come true.[55]

It is necessary to stop all outer and inner conversations—so that the voice that has actually always been there, but has been drowned out by the noise of life, can be heard. What is it trying to tell us? Professor Gruden:

> The silent encounter relativizes the words that come and fly away like thoughts and prepares our inner life to accept the richness of the unknown in which we exist and which sustains us.[56]

> The freedom is so wonderful. The silence in which there are no thoughts and no commands has freed us; freedom has come through gazing into the depths, into our own depths, in which there is no good and evil, but only what should be and also belongs there.[57]

> We will do that which spontaneously emerges as a directive from our depths, from our subconscious or—more properly stated—from our being. In the stillness, with a relaxed gaze, we will recognize with a feeling of joy where we're going and what we should do.[58]

Since 1992, Rabbi Jack Bemporad has headed the nonprofit Center for Interreligious Understanding in New York. Its goal is to bring people of all faiths together to promote open dialogue, mutual respect and a theological understanding of the common foundations of the world's religions. He is the first person in history to receive an honorary doctorate in theology from the University of St. Thomas Aquinas in Rome. In 2016, the rabbi met Braco in New York during the filming of a documentary about Braco's work in which he himself participated (the movie *The Power of Silence* is freely available on YouTube: Braco official channel). Rabbi Jack Bemporad's conclusion about Braco and his work:

People have a kind of a hunger for silence; they have a hunger to somehow be in touch with their true self. Amos has a beautiful passage; it says that there will be a hunger and a thirst. But not hunger for bread or thirst for water, but a hunger for the word of god. And that word of god, if you look at the verse [in] Kings 19, is a voice that is silent. God speaks to you through silence, but you have to be willing to listen in silence; without silence you are not going to hear it. Maybe he (Braco) represents that.[59]

The Now

But if there is no place for the present, there is no place for life, for to live is to exist, and nowhere else but in the present.[60]
Professor Vladimir Gruden, MD, PhD

People in our modern society have been fundamentally deceived by a false perception of time. By constantly thinking about their personal past and their future, many people lose sight of the present, which could provide security and all the answers that they are looking for in the past and future. Because life is what we have now. But we have to fight for the present. It doesn't come by itself, like thoughts of the past and future do. For this, it's important to cease all conversations, including the conversation with ourselves. Because words and thoughts are superfluous and unnecessary in the newly discovered present. The present is what we are, what happens around us, what we experience without definition or knowledge. Therefore, it is not important to unravel and describe what one sees. It is only important to observe the present, its invisible presence, its vibration, its being, which has no name, to perceive how it shows itself to us through feelings. Since only a few people have experienced the now, the present moment, inside themselves, the now, the present moment and its tremendous possibilities remain incomprehensible. But even those who do not cling to the past in their thoughts or engage in worrying about the future have plenty of opportunities in the course of life to miss out on the present. During most of their daily life, their thoughts are focused on the next moment, on what they still have to do or want to do. Or they're dwelling on an event in the distant future that holds the prospect of happiness or an enjoyable time: "Then life will be different and I can be happy." And with that thought in mind, life seeps away in the constant "having to do something" or in the prospect and hope of a future event. But the next moment is an illusion, a product of the imagination, because only the present really exists, the present moment. To be in the present is a special state of consciousness in which people can find everything they need. It is peace, endlessness, the feeling of being connected to everything, something eternal that is new and always pure in every moment. A feeling of being connected to something intangible. Professor Gruden expresses it in his book *Bracos Blick 2* (English: *Braco's Gaze 2*) as follows:

Let's just give ourselves up to silent wakefulness for a few minutes when we encounter Braco's gaze. We will sense existence, that which alone exists, we will feel how great and powerful the here-and-now is.[61]

As small and meaningless as it may seem, the present moment is one of the most precious things that people can find on earth: it is the personal gateway to freedom. Those who have ever sensed the now in an encounter with Braco are not willing to do without it again. But in everyday life, the present and the current moment do not give themselves to us on their own. They have to be conquered. The Croatian scientist Drago Plečko said in a lecture in the USA in 2009:

The fundamental wisdom behind what Braco does is: At every moment, we should live in the here and now! The most important fact is that somehow Braco is able to open you up for this present moment within seconds. The prerequisite is that you are at least partially ready for it. It's astonishing that such a state of mind can lead to physical recovery if the will is there.[62] If we understand that only the present moment exists and there is no past—because the past is irretrievably gone and it cannot be changed, just as little as you can change the future that is yet to come, if it comes, but it definitely does not yet exist—then we are standing on the threshold of the solution to all our problems.[63] When you are completely present, anything can happen, because you enter a phase of all possibilities, of all potential. All possibilities stand open to anyone who is present in the moment.[64]

The now, which some people experience in their encounter with Braco and his gaze, also feels like a sheltered space for emotional life. Whoever is there feels free. From there, a view of one's situation in life emerges that is usually different and much more positive than the multitude of thoughts and feelings had previously suggested. The experience of the now is only given spontaneously. You cannot compel access by force of will or plan it out with your rational mind, because you can never enter this place with your rational mind. At this level of consciousness, there is no thought as we know it in everyday life.

Those who know the now become mindful and aware in their thoughts and try to remain in the moment. This state of consciousness is more valuable than anything else. The next moment, any event in the future or the past—nothing even comes close to the value of the present moment. Aggravation, restlessness, worries, envy, despair, self-blame, feelings of guilt, fear, negative thoughts: all these inner states close the door to the now. It then seems to be unreachable. But who willingly departs from the source that can give all answers and dispel every pain? It is beyond imagining to be connected to something that is new and pure at every moment, knows no past and future, bears everything within itself and is everything. There is perfect harmony and peace. Happy are those who are able to keep the connection with the now within themselves.

In February 2020, a man attending an event with Braco in Germany confided in me about a profound experience after multiple encounters with Braco's gaze:

I can't express the feeling in words. It's like I was connected to everything at the same time. It was absolute abundance, not a hint of lacking anything. That's why there were no personal desires. I no longer had questions because this feeling contained all the answers. It sounds strange and it's so hard to put into words. I felt as if all my dreams had been fulfilled at the same time in the connection to something that contains everything within itself. A sense of satisfaction and fulfillment that took hold of my entire soul. Serenity and a feeling as if all my problems solve themselves, combined with joy and happiness. There is no thought of a past or a future;

everything is now and simultaneously, with no end in sight. It's so hard to put into words. Even just talking about it, it's no longer the same thing that I experienced. Braco gave me this special experience. I was never able to feel it before.

Such profound experiences are something remarkable, similar to the spontaneous health improvements and changes in social life after an encounter with Braco's gaze. They shed light on the potential wealth of a person's inner life. In her song 'One Moment in Time,' the singer Whitney Houston described a person's potential path on their way to the now. People go through their lives, experiencing joy and sorrow, success and failure, and with grand plans for their careers and other aspects of their lives. But sometimes the whole painstakingly constructed world collapses and you're left standing among the shattered remnants of your life. But despite everything that life brings with it, there's still something left, an opportunity that can make life truly abundant, a key to freedom: the now, hidden in every moment.[65] (You can find the original song lyrics on the internet.)

We live in a time of transition to something new. Such a time is very challenging and not easy, but also holds tremendous opportunities. When the world is changing, it's good to be ready to change too so that you can keep up with what the new situation demands. The conquest and discovery of our own inner lives appear to be among the most important necessities of our time. In his book *Das Mysterium Braco 3* (English: *The Mystery of Braco 3*), Drago Plečko quotes from a conversation with Braco:

If I stop someone in the moment, in the now, out of the reach of his mourning for the past and his fears for the future, then he will comprehend the why. And the how then comes by itself because from now on, he's guided by his spirit, that quintessence in him that is infallible. This whole process has to be spontaneous because the moment you want to influence something through your will, you start thinking about it. And when you think about it, the rational mind takes over. And we know that this rational mind, as much as we believe in it and are full of flattering praise for its scientific achievements, was also responsible for the worst atrocities in history.[66]

Chapter 3

Consciousness Comes First

Drago Plečko studied at the Faculty of Natural Sciences in Zagreb, specializing in organic chemistry and biochemistry. He graduated in 1975 with a master's degree in the chemistry of natural substances. Due to his academic background, Plečko always had problems accepting anything that lay outside of areas that had been studied, and yet he was still looking for answers to life:

> Only after meeting some people who had clearly demonstrated their abilities, and after my own intensive experiences, did I become more open to what can't be explained—which doesn't however mean that it doesn't exist.[67]

His experiences led him to a philosophy of life in which consciousness is primary and matter is secondary. Thirst for knowledge or an inner compulsion to learn more about himself and human beings' inner dimension led him to travel the world for 30 years, as described above. During his travels he met almost all the great masters, sages and teachers who were alive at the time. Plečko was the first person from the former Yugoslavia to publish interviews with Maharishi Mahesh Yogi and the Dalai Lama as well as a number of other spiritual teachers, including Vladimir Prelog, a respected Nobel Prize winner in chemistry. He took part in several hundred television and radio programs on meditation and alternative methods of healing. He is the author of several books and the first television film about the Medjugorje phenomenon. He has also been invited as a speaker to several dozen European and international conferences on the paranormal sciences. Plečko comes from Samobor, a town neighboring Zagreb. He currently lives in Zagreb. It's a particular coincidence that he came across Braco in his own country only after a 30-year spiritual quest around the globe. Since he had already gained experience with phenomena of all kinds during those years, he was convinced that he would not find anything in the encounter with Braco that he had not already seen in one form or another in his decades-long travels. But meeting Braco made such an impression on him that he spent five years accompanying him to various events and conferences. There he would give introductory lectures about Braco and his work to the audience. He published his experiences with Braco in four books in total.

Drago Plečko and His First Encounter with Braco

It's always about rejecting the worldview you have learned in some way, pushing it aside or at least opening yourself up to another principle of understanding that you haven't learned yet.[68]
Drago Plečko

It was around the time of Braco's birthday on 23 November 2004. Traditionally, several thousand visitors come to Zagreb every year for this event. Drago Plečko was on his way to a discussion when he saw the crowd waiting. In his book *Das Mysterium Braco 1* (English: *The Mystery of Braco 1*), he recollects this encounter as follows:

It is 23 November. A cool morning in Zagreb. The fruit and vegetable market on Kvaternik Square is already filled with bustling activity. You can see multiple women dragging plastic bags overflowing with soup greens and chicken legs. The small cafes are full. But people aren't stopping to chat on the street as usual because it's already too cold. Cars stop at traffic lights, waiting for a green light so they can drive up the short slope to the roundabout, where some turn right toward one of the hospitals in Zagreb, others turn left into the maze of surrounding streets. Some cars drive straight, in the direction of Srebrnjak, a placid and elegant neighborhood with one long boulevard and many old villas. At the roundabout, at the first building in Srebrnjak, a crowd has gathered. I find it difficult to estimate the size, but there are certainly several hundred people. Two uniformed police officers are nervously trying to direct traffic while buses with license plates of diverse origins try to park on Srebrnjak Street. More and more buses are arriving and the police are signaling the drivers to keep driving and find a parking space elsewhere...Everyone is holding bouquets of flowers in their hands and stepping from one foot to the other to keep warm. Evidently they've been standing here for hours, so they must have come early in the morning or even during the night. The crowd is getting bigger and bigger and more and more people want to enter the courtyard of the building at Srebrnjak 1...The crowds have already flooded the whole area, threatening to bring traffic to a standstill. The police officers have their hands full just trying to keep normal traffic going somehow. The crowd pushes its way into the courtyard, which will soon be completely overflowing, but the stream of people shows no sign of drying up. I think it's hilarious, because I live in Zagreb and don't know anyone who receives thousands of birthday well wishers. Of the people I know, I can't think of anyone who could attract so many people, not even if they were paid to come. But someone is able to, someone they call "Braco" of all things, like a boy from my neighborhood in Samobor where I grew up...

"We all call him Braco," replies an old woman from Zagorje, somewhat indignant at my provocation. "He saved my little boy, he was a drinker. They treated him in the hospital and nothing came of it. I brought him to Braco and he hasn't drunk a drop since. Now he's completely normal. For two years now." As if she had read my thoughts, the old woman turned her head to me and lectured me in a shrill voice: "My son, you have no idea who Braco is. He's not a medicine man or anything like that. He looks like a little boy, but he can do things no one else can. He's helped so many and continues to help people. Would thousands bring flowers to his birthday each year if it weren't so? We aren't so foolish that someone could convince us of something that doesn't exist. Everyone is clever enough to know for themselves how much something has helped them. The people who weren't helped certainly aren't here now." I wondered why I had never heard anything about this person, who over the course of the day will welcome around 10,000 people.[69]

Drago Plečko

A friend of Drago Plečko who worked for Croatian television facilitated a personal meeting with Braco. Plečko also describes it in his first book:

In front of me stood a thirty-seven year old man with a gentle smile and a relaxed look. He is of medium height and his voice is very soft and soothing. Long straight hair falls to his shoulders and he is dressed very simply. He wore a white shirt with a Russian collar and gray trousers. He asked us to be seated and we were served coffee, cake, chocolates and even cigarettes. After exchanging a few sentences, it became clear I was dealing with a highly educated native of Zagreb who, as I later learned, had completed a master's degree in business administration. He reads widely, is up to date with recent literature in his field and doesn't try to dominate the conversation. To be honest, I was surprised by the humility of a man to whose birthday thousands of people come as if he were a saint. As if sensing what I was thinking, he smiled and said: "Authority is not gained through violence, but through love and compassion." I learn that there are seventy-two cassettes and DVDs about Braco, each two hours long, on which people share experiences they've had during Braco's sessions. Nearly 150 hours of film footage with reports providing more or less convincing evidence of his healing powers. There are stories of improved health, the supposed healing of cancer, heart disease, apoplexy, paralysis, childhood illnesses, leukemia, multiple sclerosis, drug addiction and a whole range of other diseases, mental disorders, marital problems, bad parent-child relationships, up to and including financial problems. This material has been recorded over the past nine years, ever since Braco took the helm at 1 Srebrnjak Street.

It's almost incomprehensible that a person about whom such incredible stories are told—he can heal people just by touching their photographs, or he can change other people's lives within a few minutes—can be so humble and relaxed, and he never gives the impression of being an overbearing person who expects special treatment. My impression was more that there was something childlike in him. He laughed heartily at every witty provocation or an ingenious joke at his expense, and at no time did he try to prove that the legends about him were true and the gossip was all a lie.[70]

Attending International Conferences

In November 2006, Drago Plečko presented Braco at one of the world's largest international congresses for consciousness and healing, the Basel PSI conference. Around 100 healers, scientists and other experts were on the congress's list of speakers. To the great astonishment of the congress directors, 3000 of the 3300 attendees at this highly renowned conference came to the events with Braco and his gaze. One of the main organizers of the congress, the German psychologist Dr. Harald Wiesendanger, known for his extensive publications on the subject of spiritual healing, spoke about Braco at the conference:

> I've studied spiritual healing for more than 15 years and have met well over 1000 healers in person, and Braco was invited here because in my personal impression, he's actually an exception among these 1000.[71]

Austrian television became aware of Braco through the congress. In spring 2007, Austria's national broadcaster ORF invited Braco onto the television program *Primavera*. The show was broadcast in prime time and was moderated by Dr. Verena Russwurm. Drago Plečko, together with a medical colleague, explained Braco's working method and his special gift to an Austrian audience. Appearances in many Austrian cities and further invitations to expos followed, which attracted a large number of participants. In April 2008, Drago Plečko accompanied Braco to an international congress on consciousness in Italy. Here, too, they encountered auditoriums with every seat filled.

The Beginning in the USA

Finally, among the many events of the time, I would like to single out Braco's first invitation to the USA in 2009. Together with Drago Plečko, Braco went to Laughlin, Nevada, for an international conference on the paranormal sciences and consciousness, which was also attended by experts. Drago Plečko introduced Braco to an American audience in a detailed presentation, which is printed in full in one of his books (*Das Mysterium Braco 3*). Here, too, Braco's gaze elicited unexpectedly positive reactions from the more than 1000 people who had found a seat in the main hall of the conference hotel, even though none of them had met him before. Among other things, Drago Plečko reports that a man from Colorado who had barely been able to walk for more than two years due to pain from advanced rheumatoid arthritis was quickly freed of all his ailments. Braco's events at this conference took place daily for eight days and were always fully booked. The conference was followed by invitations to every corner of the USA. From 2010 to 2014, Braco visited 44 different cities in 21 states. He regularly toured from coast to coast to respond to all those who had invited him. In several DVDs, a camera team documented testimonials from visitors who came in their thousands.

"The guru who has nothing to say," was how he was described in the media. There was coverage in many newspapers and magazines and on major television networks. In some places, Braco was invited back again and again because of the tremendous reception he received. In addition to the events in America, invitations to Russia, Japan, and Australia soon followed. In every country, no matter what culture he encountered, Braco stood silently in the same way for a few minutes on the stage and gazed at the large groups. He never spoke even a single word in public. What was given to him as a gift in May 1995 never deserted him. Although he made no effort to have an effect, the special energy could be felt in the hall as soon as he began to lift his eyes in order to gaze at the groups of people. It naturally kept flowing out of him without ceasing whenever he imparted his gaze. He just let it happen.

It's a Pure Gift

In his books, Drago Plečko compares Braco's work to that of some of the most prominent spiritual figures.

> History records great yogis who were able to enlighten their disciples with just their gaze without speaking a single word. It's not about how it's done, but who does it. The Vedic scriptures state that there were masters who could do this without their disciples being nearby. One who is in any way connected with this common consciousness, the collective consciousness, can accomplish almost anything. But on principle, it's not talked about. One of the greatest Advaita Vedanta philosophers of all time—Ramana Maharshi—is said to have never spoken. He lived on the slopes of the Himalayas and during his life composed only forty verses, which were meant to show the path to flee from this human existence. For him, that said everything there was to be said. The reason he didn't speak was because he had recognized that his knowledge couldn't be conveyed in words anyway.[72]

In India, eye contact (looking and being seen) with a spiritually advanced person is of particular importance. People in India have known for a long time that just through the gaze or presence of a yogi who has achieved inner mastery, the heart opens, blessings and divine energy are given, and healing can also occur. Some people want to explain Braco's gift as being the result of decades of meditation or yoga practice. Thus he is compared to masters from the Far East who meditated or lived in seclusion for their entire lives. However, as mentioned above, Braco doesn't engage in any form of spiritual practice. He doesn't meditate, live in isolation, or follow any spiritual tradition. He has never in his life been interested in spiritual topics. He spent the first two decades of his life living like many other young people. As the only child of a prosperous family, he had access to all the benefits of the modern age. It wasn't until May 1995, after the unexpected death of his predecessor and best friend Ivica Prokić, that Braco's gift spontaneously appeared. In Drago Plečko's view, Braco's consciousness awakened on its own when he started on his predetermined path. Others believe that this was when his special gift was bestowed on him by God. In his book *Das Mysterium Braco 1* (English: *The Mystery of Braco 1*), Drago Plečko offers his view:

> In what this silent healer does, there is no logic, no scientific justification, no religious or suggestive elements, no form of hypnosis, no methods that are known from other traditions we're familiar with, no startling tricks and no electronic devices or sounds that could carry a subliminal message. There's nothing that can be used to explain the effect on the organism of another person, let alone on their fate.[73]

As becomes clear in the course of the book, Braco has remained a human being despite the thousands of people who find their way to him. Not only Drago Plečko, but also others who got to know him better, were impressed by the modesty and naturalness of his nature. It is a rarity in our very ego-centered times that a person who is so popular and respected does not succumb to conceit. I was able to observe it again and again: he can rejoice and marvel like a child, and even in difficult situations his special joy of life remains. On the other hand, I always saw a great seriousness and personal sacrifice when it comes to people who seek help through his gift.

Dr. William Tiller, professor emeritus at Stanford University, invited Braco together with Drago Plečko to his home in Arizona on their first visit to the USA in 2009. Professor Tiller was and is an icon of consciousness research in the USA. Through his research, he developed and proved the idea that our consciousness can change the so-called physical reality of our lives. This means that the human spirit, human consciousness, can influence matter and space. Professor Tiller and other researchers recognized that human beings are much more and can do much more than we have thought possible. Professor Tiller was so impressed by Braco's mode of operation that he wanted to meet him in person. His concise comment on the rather unusual way Braco works—namely through his gaze—is:

The least important [thing] is the way in which one affects this network of interconnected dots of Reality. What matters are the results.[74]

Professor Tiller sees Braco, as mentioned at the beginning, as the leading figure of the new paradigm.[75]

Chapter 4

The Goal and Purpose of Life Must Always Be Happiness

With some people, their inner potential is asleep. They live on the surface. The play of words and thoughts is difficult to understand. This play thrives on the past, which is often connected to feelings of guilt and an uncertain, worrying future because you don't know what's coming. Due to our upbringing and painful experiences, our mental world is often shaped by negative thoughts and feelings. Doubt predominates instead of trust and optimism since there's no solid footing to really provide support. This support can only come from the invisible, from the inner life, which needs to be tended like a flower that needs sun, water and fertilizer to grow. Our inner life, which can be revitalized through the energy in Braco's gaze, needs our attention, silence and energy in order to live again. The feelings of love, peace, joy and optimism coming from us are the first signs of an awakening.[76]
Professor Vladimir Gruden, MD, PhD

He Showed Great Respect for Braco's Work

Professor Vladimir Gruden graduated in 1963 from the medical school of the University of Zagreb, where he later became a full professor of medical psychology. He was also a medical specialist in psychiatry. For decades, his practical work and scientific research focused on psychotherapy. He was well known in Croatia thanks to his television and radio appearances. As a lecturer he was involved in the training and continuing education of students and physicians, and he wrote around 20 books, including works for both scholarly and popular audiences. Professor Gruden's scientific research was also reflected in his participation as a speaker at numerous conferences, both in

Croatia and internationally. He participated in several projects for the Croatian Ministry of Science and Education and the World Health Organization. He co-authored several textbooks on psychiatry and psychological medicine and also mentored numerous theses, master's degrees and doctoral dissertations. In addition, he was president of the Croatian psychotherapy association and a member of many national and international societies. His statements were often cited as expert opinion in the Croatian media.

Over the last few years, I met this man repeatedly. He impressed me with his positive charisma. In conversation, he was both humorous and thoughtful. I soon felt that this professor of medicine was one of those who understood the soul and its richness. He showed great respect for Braco's work, which at first he only observed for years until, convinced at last, he publicly advocated for Braco in lectures and also in print and broadcast media until his death in January 2020. Professor Gruden:

> For years, as a scientist, I have been curious to hear about the changes that take place in people when they encounter Braco's gaze. I wanted to compare it to what I've seen in medicine, especially in psychiatry, which is my area of expertise. In my experience, it's of great importance for people in need of help to have confidence that they can get better, and I have found that Braco has the ability to arouse that confidence in people...Everyone is searching for the truth in some way. There are different schools of thought, people with different worldviews, sects, groups, communities, many of which proudly proclaim their own views about truth. This is a subjective truth. Yet all are striving to find real, objective truth. As for Braco, many people are enthusiastic about him, while others dispute his abilities. But his existence is extremely important for many people. For a great many. This fact alone draws our attention

to him. So what is it that fascinates people about Braco and sets him apart from others? How close has Braco come to the truth? Why are so many people so fascinated by him, regardless of their attitude to life, their worldview or their origin? Truth is what it is and not what we think it is, what we wish for or what we stubbornly insist on. Regardless of how much what exists differs from our wishes, we cannot close our eyes to what really is.[77]

At the events with Braco, especially in Croatia and Slovenia, Professor Gruden prepared the audience for the experience with Braco and his gaze. As mentioned above, he wrote many scientific books during the course of his life, but my impression is that his last two works, *Bracos Blick 1* and *Bracos Blick 2* (English: *Braco's Gaze 1* and *Braco's Gaze 2*), had a special significance for him. Here he applied his decades of experience as an acknowledged expert in the field of psychotherapy to approach the phenomenon of Braco and his gift. The result is a work that is able to meet scientific standards. He clearly put not only his expertise but also his whole heart into the two books. At the end of his second book, he writes:

I thank you for putting me on this path and for always making me aware of the values I've come across on it and the words with which I've described it all. I implore you that all that has been written here might prove useful to people in their search for happiness, peace and truth. And I thank you, no matter what your name is or what you are called. After everything we have witnessed and gone through in our encounter with Braco, we have gained the experience of frequently calling out: God, the unknown in me, the boundless self—I give myself to you—give me strength, awaken me, give me to myself! This entire book could be summarized with two words: wakeful silence. From many points of view and using many examples, this book highlighted and demonstrated how valuable it is to put an end to every discussion (with others or with yourself) and to keep our attention on experiencing the answers from the depths of our inner being. The encounter with Braco is exactly this: the encounter with the wakeful (the gaze) stillness (the silence).[78]

It's a fact, according to Professor Gruden, that Braco has the ability to improve the lives of those who attend his events through his gaze. How does he do that? Much remains unknown. At an encounter with Braco, events occur that we only partially understand. In studying visitors' experiences, you repeatedly hear of an energy that emanates from Braco. In the words of Professor Gruden:

At this encounter, the majority of people have the experience of being exposed to an energy. They feel this energy flowing through their bodies. Some of them sway back and forth, not a few begin to weep and the majority are overtaken by a feeling of liberation. It's a liberation from something undefined. From a psychoanalytical perspective, it's probably the resolution of an internal psychic conflict of undefined content. Nor does it need to be defined. This conflict involves emotional anguish, not mental anguish. Something good from outside expels this bad from within us.[79]

The Unknown

Man must gradually come to terms with the idea of possessing something that he does not understand and that is beyond his comprehension. We are not only what we know about ourselves. We are much, much more.[80]

Professor Vladimir Gruden, MD, PhD

The American camera team documented a striking report from an attendee in Hawaii:

My mother is 97 and had been on her deathbed for four months and lost a lot of weight. She had large sores on her body because she couldn't move and only lay in bed, although she was well cared for. There was no way she could get any better because she kept losing weight. It started with pneumonia and then she got MRSA, an antibiotic-resistant germ. And it was in her mouth. It was infected and she couldn't eat. I was with her on a Thursday. That same day a friend called me and invited me to an event with Braco's gaze online. I went. I had forgotten my mother's photo, but I was thinking of her with all my heart. Then the next day I visited my mother in the hospital and she was walking down the hall using a walker and with a nurse on each side. My god, it was a miracle! The nurses told me she had gotten up that morning and wanted to walk and have breakfast. All she had eaten for a month was a small cup with something in it. It was incredible and the nurses all came up to me and said, "Your mother's been given a new life. Something happened. She got up this morning, we don't know what happened."[81]

In Germany a visitor shared the following after an event with Braco:

I've suffered from bronchial asthma for over 35 years. At first I only had attacks in the summer, but for the last 12 years they've been occurring year round. Eight weeks after my fourth visit to a session with Braco, I asked Braco in my mind to help me with my asthma. That evening, my asthma disappeared. I can walk through freshly cut hay without a reaction. I don't need the sprays anymore that I had to take.[82]

Who or what works through Braco's gaze? How does his gaze reach so many people and give help? How can it be that merely having a mental connection with him or watching a film about him is enough to experience improvements in life? Why does Braco attract thousands of people when he does nothing on the outside? What is it that he gives through his gaze that can change people so much and obviously lift them inwardly to what experts call a higher level of being human? Professor Gruden:

> The secret lies in what he provides, and what he provides is the unknown. That is simultaneously nothing but also a great deal, even the greatest thing that can be given, only it cannot be defined. The unknown has no material form. It cannot be expressed in words. Easily and without notice, it overcomes all boundaries and, just as unnoticed, gains entrance into the hopes and desires of all people, regardless of their natures or their political or philosophical convictions.[83]

This unknown dimension of life is invisible, but it's part of life, the essence of life, life itself. It is always around us, but also within us. It is what constitutes our innermost being. It is the unknown in people that encounters itself again in the unknown that touches and changes people through the gaze of Braco. Whoever approaches the forgotten part of our psyche soon feels that it's not just about the unknown, an invisible level of life or an energy, but that behind it all is the unknown. It is the unknown that has already left much evidence of its existence in the visible world, from the beauty and diversity of nature to the grandeur of outer space with its wonders. It is also hidden in the innermost part of every human soul, often beneath so many layers and veils, seemingly inaccessible to human consciousness. Professor Gruden:

We accept the existence of something that is unknown and undefined. The advantage lies in the recognition that the unknown exists here, right next to us. And that's enough, because that's all you can attribute to the unknown.[84]

Let's discard the obsession with having to understand everything, know everything, define everything. We should make friends with the unknown. The unknown is only invisible to our rational mind.[85]

The more we try to understand or define the unknown, the smaller it becomes. The unknown is greater the less it is known, the less we explore it or try to describe it. We need only the strength and inner peace to accept that it cannot be grasped or held. The unknown is known to the unknown dimension of our being.[86]

In the stillness, together with the gaze, we seem to feel the opening of a hidden door that gives us insight into a previously unknown world.[87]

The correct path lies only in wakeful silence. This is why we remain silent and observe. The truth that's right before our eyes only comes to us in wakeful silence.[88]

People should turn more to the unknown dimension within them. This may be difficult and unfamiliar at first, but it's important just to start. Depending on tradition and culture, the term "the unknown" could also be replaced by "the innermost part of the soul," "the spark from the light of God," "God within us," "the true self," or a similar term. But these words are only labels that do not evoke real understanding. Words and terms quickly trigger negative or positive emotions, depending on one's upbringing and life experience. Any description of the indescribable is more or less wrong. This area of life can only be experienced. Those who present a personal image, a mental explanation, as the truth are distancing themselves from reality. It is far better to help people and show them ways to find the connection within themselves, so that they achieve personal experiences firsthand, than to tell them with words or dictate to them how it is. Those who begin to feel it know immediately that there are no words to describe it. This touch is an inexpressible feeling that hits a person in the innermost part and leaves them speechless and stunned. One can only surrender to the unknown and approach it in silence. Professor Gruden:

> Why should we not smile when we have found our unknown self, connected it with the known I, and thus realized the wholeness of existence?[89]

Getting to know your own inner life changes who you are as a person. You find new strength, happiness and, above all, peace. By uniting our known self with the unknown self, we achieve the wholeness of existence.

The Encounter with the True Self

After an event in the USA, when asked what Braco and his work meant to them, two visitors said:

> He's obviously able to purify people from within. Through the experience, they become a clear channel for the source. If someone can do that, it's just amazing, it's incredible.[90]

> I just call it an extraordinary change, so that each of us is able to search our feelings and find out who we really are without the accumulated junk of our habits. We are what we have always wanted.[90]

It is the changes in the inner lives of some people who come to events with Braco that are reminiscent of an inner awakening. Something in their inner lives is enlivened and ignited, like a spark that has only glowed for a long time and then suddenly becomes brighter and breaks into flame for the first time. For some visitors, this change can be directly experienced and is also described that way. In addition, often strong uplifting feelings are perceived without external cause, "just popping up from within," as one visitor described it. Is this increasing brightness inside in connection with these beautiful feelings a sign that something is awakening in us that has been asleep for a long time? Perhaps these beautiful feelings that are simply there, without any apparent cause, are the natural qualities of our soul, of our true self: happiness, joy, peace, love. But everybody is different. Some people need a little time, others a much longer time, to start to feel themselves in this touching manner. And still others cannot perceive any changes in themselves. But those who feel the emerging brightness in their souls through the energy in Braco's gaze direct their view inward. As a visitor once said to me, it's like the glow of the morning sun that penetrates the mist and makes the inner life brighter and brighter. As already mentioned at the beginning, it seems to be a goal of the encounters with Braco and his gaze to make people familiar with themselves again and to give them a connection to their own soul, to their true selves. In the sound recording of his voice (see also Chapter 7), Braco says:

People tend to believe in what they see—in the body, and therefore respect each other according to criteria such as skin color, appearance, gender, religion or faith. And often we forget what is inside us. We forget that invisible spark that makes us happy or sad, tired or rested. And I try to help your sparks to ignite more and more, to glow, to flare up to a flame that will warm you even more...Let's start thinking about ourselves, but not only about our body, but also about this spark that is in it...Respect your spark, which is called soul and which has life in it. I, Braco, will be there for you whenever you wish it, and I will try to illuminate the path on which you are walking with the desire to make you acquainted with yourself.[91]

After an event with Braco at a large expo in Hamburg, the director asked me what Braco was doing so that so many people in the hall were simply happy after just a few minutes of his gaze. This striking experience has repeated itself again and again after events with Braco, whether in the USA, Russia, Japan, Australia, in other European countries or in any of the 30 countries he has visited in the last two decades. Many of the people who leave the hall have a smile on their face. They seem to radiate from within. As previously mentioned, Braco's gaze brings some people a feeling of relief in their soul that cannot be precisely explained. Something is simply no longer there that was there before and caused a heaviness in their soul. After a few minutes of Braco's gaze, it has fallen away. What is it that has disappeared? Maybe it's not so important to know that; the only important thing is this special feeling that suddenly becomes palpable for some visitors, that arises in them after something else has been taken away. So often, I have seen tears of relief when the new becomes palpable inside. Today, in a time of numerous problems and serious faces, it's just liberating to feel joy and happiness again. Just to see life with different eyes again. Despite personal problems and the seemingly insurmountable challenges constantly repeated in the media, life bursts into bloom from within. When the inner life has become bright again, the soul again sees—through human eyes—the world's beauty that has never left us. Here are some additional examples of internal changes following the experience of Braco's gaze taken from reports of people attending events in Europe:

A current through the body, a feeling of happiness, a sense of fulfillment. When I come here, I'm really happy.[92]

I come to Braco and feel joy in my heart. The many questions I asked have become unimportant. I just feel happy. When you are happy, everything works out so well.[92]

This is my fifth time there, and the love and warmth, it's a dream. I feel really happy when I'm there.[92]

It was like I was floating. I felt a bliss. Something infinite. It was very beautiful.[92]

I don't know, no amount of money in the world can pay for this. I just don't have the words; that's how happy I am.[92]

In Braco, visitors to the events meet a person whose basic personality trait is happiness. For him, the encounters with his gaze are associated with a feeling of happiness. The gaze, as some visitors perceive it, is filled with love and hope:

What I've noticed since coming to Braco is that I started to really love all the people around me.[93]

So I took it upon myself to open my heart at least for five minutes to this man who just looks at people in silence. During the encounter, I felt so much love as I could never have imagined—a pure love. I felt loved. That very day, all the pain fell away from me.[93]

Love and a special kind of joy came out of him.[93]

Authority and an incredible love and an incredible humility that moved me deeply.[93]

I felt very, very much love and warmth and my heart opened very wide. To feel that love is quite fantastic; it's like going for a swim in a warm ocean.[93]

Happiness, love, hope, optimism—there is obviously so much in the silent gaze of a man who has been sharing his special gift with people for more than two decades. No one, not even he himself, is able to give an explanation for the effect his gaze has on people. But at the end of the day, many happy and satisfied people leave his events on four continents of this earth and globally in the live stream.

Surrender

The consciousness of the person taking part in my session should be like water in free fall and simply follow its natural course. I understand that people want to have their own difficulties and problems solved as quickly as possible, but there is a law that says that nothing happens without a reason, and that everything that needed a certain amount of time to develop also takes a certain amount of time to cease existing.[94]
Braco in a conversation with Drago Plečko

The golden key on the inner path is surrender. Professor Gruden very frequently mentions this inner attitude in his books. In the same way, he once said to me in a personal conversation: "A central insight for me is the enormous importance of surrender for human life." For Professor Gruden, surrender means total freedom. There is nothing more valuable. Surrender does not mean accepting a miserable life situation. It is always only surrender to the present moment, to everything that we feel and perceive in and around us in this moment. We accept the now as it currently presents itself, with all its thoughts, feelings, conclusions, fears and ideas, just as it is, without internal resistance or any form of evaluation or interpretation. We surrender to the now, the present moment—not as a victim but in the knowledge that, through doing so, a path to help and liberation can be opened. Surrender is letting go. It frees us from attachments and lets us again become children who surrender in order to be able to accept help.

In 2009, as said above, Drago Plečko traveled with Braco to a major scientific congress in the USA. In his introductory presentation before Braco's appearance, he said:

> It takes some time to understand the idea of "let it happen." The key word is time. All chemical processes have a time sequence. We imagine all problems chronologically, and most things will happen in the future, that is, in time. However, it seems that some people who accepted the guidance of their inner feeling of "let it happen" were healed during the "encounter" with Braco's gaze, sometimes even instantaneously. Because outside of time, everything is possible.[95]
>
> (Complete presentation reprinted in the book *Das Mysterium Braco 3* by Drago Plečko)

Surrender is a strong protection of our inner life against the constant attacks and assaults of negative thoughts and feelings, which will destroy the stillness in the soul if we take them in and believe them. Surrender helps open the door to the qualities of inner life. Getting to know the inner life is not a conscious and logical way of knowing, but a kind of melding, a kind of immersion. It is a direct, immediate experience. It cannot be expressed in words. In this way, according to Professor Gruden, we come to know ourselves and God and have our first experiences with the unknown that constitutes our life. In his book *Bracos Blick 1* (English: *Braco's Gaze 1*), Professor Gruden writes:

The solution lies in accepting what is and in surrendering yourself to the experiences that occur without evaluating them. What is, is; what I feel, I feel; what I experience, I experience.[96]

The most important decision is just to surrender ourselves. We surrender to ourselves and to everything that is happening around us and within us at this moment. We surrender ourselves to the present moment. And in doing so, we feel that we are alive, that we exist.[97]

There is no wisdom or knowledge that can compete with surrender. Surrendering ourselves to this immensity that encompasses us frees us from all worries and feelings of fear.[98]

We feel the courage to embrace the unknown. The dispelling of our doubts is not found in any wise maxims, but in surrender, in trust and in the conviction that we are able to and want to lead our lives in a way that makes us happy. Because happiness, as we already know, is the meaning of life.[99]

Optimism

Many people in our modern times live with the feeling or even the certainty that their lives are difficult. There's no doubt that people face great challenges today. But apart from manifestly external factors, feelings about the quality of one's personal life seem to be highly dependent on the inner life of each individual. "Mental suffering, suffering in the soul, is the greatest suffering," a wise man said, and he is right. For many people, a heaviness or even pain in the soul is a reality. This is where doctors have a hard time helping. A mental heaviness makes everything in life turn gray. It's like carrying weights that pull the soul down. In such a condition, optimism seems divorced from reality, unattainable, irrational and naive. Spiritual suffering is often associated with unpleasant memories, doubts about the success of personal plans, and distrust in one's own abilities and qualities. But who can remember that happiness and optimism are fundamental characteristics of life? The noise of countless words, thoughts and conversations, both external and internal, does not allow us to remember happiness or to turn consciously toward optimism. Optimism and a liberated, happy inner life free of burdens seem to be a gift only enjoyed by children. But this, as Professor Gruden writes in his books, is the result of foolish habits and a flawed upbringing dominated by worries.[100] We haven't learned to be happy. A child's trust, incomprehensible to reason and logic, is lost over the years under the influence of constant parental worries and an upbringing and education that places little value in the formation and strengthening of the inner life. Thus, in many cases, pessimism comes to replace optimism and zest for life as the predominant feeling. Life comes to be guided more and more by reason and logic. Since life is unpredictable, reason and logic can't exist without fear and anxiety. We can counter each sad thought with a positive one, such as: "This will turn out in a constructive and positive way for me." But it's surprisingly difficult to overcome pessimism.

Braco and Professor Gruden, 2015

In the encounter with Braco, visitors expect something positive, something new, to happen. Something that will help them to be happy again. In the stillness with his gaze, some people experience the inner triumph of optimism. Inner silence seems to be a foundation for the rise of optimism. In the emerging inner stillness, it's often present as the predominant feeling. A man described to me his experience during his encounter with Braco's gaze:

> I felt a space of stillness and emptiness inside me. After a short time, it seemed to be filled with optimism and confidence. This feeling of optimism was simply there, like air for breathing. It came from deep inside me. I couldn't help but be optimistic. It was followed by a feeling of joy.[101]

Optimism is one of the basic sensations of our inner life. Professor Gruden describes it as a collective universal feeling that is firmly rooted in the entirety of existence. As already mentioned elsewhere, some of those who attend events with Braco report feeling an inner liberation that leads to silence in their consciousness. The emptiness in consciousness resulting from the absence of thought helps the qualities of the soul, the innermost part of every person, become naturally perceptible. Feelings of optimism, joy and happiness that have no basis in external life suddenly appear. There are no longer questions or doubts about the beauty of life.[101] The experience is often associated with a profound sense of peace and the feeling of being protected, sheltered and secure.[101] Professor Gruden:

> Optimism is an integral part of our existence and has nothing to do with mysticism. We only need to approach optimism with complete calmness of mind and concentration. There can be no paths of pessimism in these encounters because a kind of awakening is taking place here. In the right atmosphere, it is an awakening from a dream full of suffering and doubt.[102]

Nothingness

Everything happens in stillness, without words. And in this stillness, in this seeming nothingness, there is everything. In stillness, happiness and the meaning of life are dominant.[103]
Professor Vladimir Gruden, MD, PhD

We human beings are generally accustomed to seeing strength and grandeur in expressions of external power. But perhaps this view is only correct when looking at our three-dimensional world where external things predominate. *The Power of Silence,*[104] a documentary about Braco's life and work, begins with a quotation from the Old Testament. The words relate to the prophet Elijah (1 Kings 19:10–13). At a time of severe persecution, he was gripped with despair and felt alone. Because of this, he sought refuge in a cave.

He was told, "Go out and stand on the mountain before the Lord, for the Lord is about to pass by." The biblical account continues:

Now there was a great wind, so strong that it was splitting mountains and breaking rocks in pieces before the Lord, but the Lord was not in the wind; and after the wind an earthquake, but the Lord was not in the earthquake; and after the earthquake a fire, but the Lord was not in the fire; and after the fire a gentle whisper. When Elijah heard it, he wrapped his face in his mantle and went out and stood at the entrance of the cave.

A few years ago, I was talking to a friend. We talked about life and its meaning, the inner path, and the meaning of the present time. I then asked him what the greatest goal was that he wanted to achieve in his life. As an answer, I expected the realization of selfless love, humility, union with my soul, happiness, inner freedom or similar. But his answer pierced my heart and touched something that is difficult to describe. There was only one word, but to this day I still cannot forget it. He said: "Nothingness." At first I couldn't understand what is so desirable about achieving nothingness as a state of mind, but through my experiences with Braco's gaze I have been coming to understand it more and more.

The wisdom of many religions and teachings speaks of everything that is truly great being often small and unimpressive in appearance. In fact, the right solution lies in an almost unexpected simplicity. What Braco provides is evidently nothing: he comes, places himself in front of crowds of people at events and conferences, asks nothing, says nothing, gazes — and leaves. But this nothingness is the result of our senses' very limited ability to perceive things. It is good to accept this so-called nothing as something, even if we cannot define and understand it. It takes a while to realize that a nothing can be something after all. Visitors open themselves to something they cannot see or hear, trusting that it exists. This step is necessary because it is a step from the visible and mental fullness of our present plane of life into the apparent nothingness of another higher plane of life. This step is made possible, however, by the energy in Braco's gaze. Professor Gruden:

> Let us mutually unite in the conviction that nothingness represents an empty shell for consciousness. Since we are not accustomed to thinking like this, we are too weak for the step into nothingness. Braco's courage and determination to observe us in silence and repeat this step countless times also encourages us to believe in this nothingness more than in anything else.[105]

> Let us accept this so-called nothingness. We will not understand it, but we will feel the dimensions of the invisible.[106]

The Soul

The inner life of many people, their soul, is trapped in an almost impenetrable shell, a cocoon or a net, formed by the energy of a multitude of negative thoughts and feelings, inner conflicts and an overload of unnecessary information. Thus, human beings are separated from themselves in their consciousness and remain impressionable and can be easily deceived. They lack the ability to distinguish the good from the bad, the building up from the breaking down, the positive from the negative. The soul has this ability, but the mind is limited. This is an important cause of the misfortunes in one's personal life and indeed of the unfortunate situation in the whole world. The existence of the soul as a separate consciousness, independent of the body, is still a foreign concept to some people. It seems easier to believe that the soul and mental sensations are only part of the body, an expression of special abilities, and properties of the brain and nerves that communicate through electrical impulses, hormones and specially built proteins. The body is visible and therefore real to the external senses, whereas the soul is invisible and so seems unreal. The soul is, as already mentioned in the course of the book, only perceptible in its qualities through feeling. Those who believe that the material is the basis of life do not need faith. They will not be able to accept the primacy of the soul in life. Every person defines for themselves what is primary and what is secondary in them. Where is the priority in life? Is it working on oneself to improve one's inner life, one's thoughts and feelings and behaviors? Is it the search for the soul and the origin of life, the Creator from which everything came into being? Or do the inner circumstances and values seem to be without much importance for a good life, and only the visible and the material counts? But what is the use of knowing and having a lot if you have not understood all your life who you really are?

Life takes place to a large extent between mind and soul. Who takes the lead in life? Which voice is listened to and who is believed? The ability to hear one's own soul is given to people in different degrees, some more, some less. To those who hear it, it sometimes seems as if a voice within them is saying: *This is exactly what you have to do.* But this voice is very quiet. Life is a chain of endless choices. This choice is an expression of the freedom of a human being to believe and do what he or she thinks is right, and this shapes a person's life. By the consequences of someone's choices, one can often tell what influence they have followed. Many people follow the voice of their mind throughout their life. Everything that their soul tells them, they reject. But often it turns out that their soul knows more than their mind. It is very bitter, but also instructive, to have to admit this to oneself afterwards. Nowadays, intelligence is measured, among other things, by the ability to successfully pass corresponding tests. But isn't there also an intelligence that is measured by the ability to distinguish the true from the false? It shows itself in the ability to analyze the knowledge gained by the soul in an appropriate form. The more correct the evaluation is, the higher the intelligence. It is not often known that the main thing in a human being is their soul, and the brain is only an instrument that, if you want to put it this way, plays the necessary melodies for the soul.

Happiness is the "product" of the soul and not of the body. If we think back to the few moments in life when we have felt true happiness, they are always connected with a shaking of the spirit. Love, tenderness toward a child, delight at the beauty of nature, an opportunity to please our loved ones. No expensive purchase and no career success can cause the same comprehensive shaking of the soul. The soul carries the knowledge of the invisible world within itself and has insights that are not possible for the mind. Confidence in the existence of the invisible world, the spiritual world that can give help in every situation of life, comes from the soul. This trust is much stronger than faith, which is full of doubts, or blind faith.

Blind faith is mostly an influence or self-suggestion and does not arise from a conscious recognition. It fights everything around it that does not submit to it. The reality of life is a great knowledge that comes from the world of the invisible and is comprehended by the soul and not by the human mind, which is limited in its abilities. Quite a number of people consciously separate knowledge from feelings, and this is wrong. Faith is the knowledge of the soul. Faith as knowledge and knowledge as faith are the cornerstones of the human soul.

The task of every human being in the world boils down to being able to love. However, no human being can love by himself or herself; only the soul is capable of it. That is why it is necessary to find ways to ignite the spark in the soul, to enliven the inner being. Through these inner changes, one begins to understand what life really is. Feelings like envy, hatred, despair extinguish the light in the soul. However, finding the right path in life is often very painful, because today's world does not give confirmation of the existence of the invisible world from which help can come. Thus, the feeling of being abandoned by everything good, or if you belong to a religion, by God, quickly arises. One must open the eyes of one's soul in order to gain knowledge and be able to set clear goals for one's life. The mere existence of a sublime goal in life makes a person happy. Whoever has experienced an extraordinary touch through the connection with their soul, and acknowledges it, has experienced a moment in which their consciousness has united with their soul. It is sad that such special moments are so rare in human life. Some people do not even know what they are. But those who have experienced this agonizing happiness, even once, rarely lose their way in life again. This happiness remains in their consciousness. They can be cheerful, no matter what happens. Difficulties in life can rob us of happy moments, but it is important not to lose them. Joy destroys sadness in the soul, which ruins a person. Happiness attracts good things. The ability to laugh with joy—this is what people have forgotten. First, we should laugh at ourselves and then rejoice in all that touches our hearts. Find a reason to laugh and you will feel strength flowing in. But it is hard nowadays, as many people are wrapped up in depression.

"Listen to your soul"—this advice can be heard in all spiritual traditions. To follow it is the basic condition for a happy life. The time for oneself, the time to meet oneself, has a great importance for every human being. Perhaps being alone with oneself in this way is one of the most important and crucial experiences. You have to be alone to find out what supports you when you find that you cannot support yourself. The encounter with one's inner self, one's soul, as one can experience in the encounter with Braco and his gaze, is the basic concern of every human life. Psychologists and doctors who have found wisdom in their work make this known again and again. The world-famous Swiss psychiatrist and psychotherapist Professor C. G. Jung found very touching words to describe his personal path to his own soul:

My soul, where are you? Do you hear me? I speak, I call you—are you there? I have returned, I am here again. I have shaken the dust of all lands from my feet, and I have come to you, I am with you. After long years of wandering, I have come to you again...Do you remember me? How long our separation lasted! And how did I find you? In what words shall I tell you on what winding paths a good star has led me to you? Give me your hand, my almost forgotten soul. How warm the joy to see you again, you long denied soul. Life has led me back to you. Let us give thanks to the life I have lived, for all the happy hours and all the sad hours, for every joy, for every sadness. My soul, my journey shall continue with you. I will walk with you and rise to my silent height.[107]

Professor Gruden once expressed during the latter part of his life that he saw a very bright future for humanity. He believed that optimism and happiness would become more and more widespread in the time to come. The whole universe and nature exist only because of happiness. The entire creation, in its beauty, shows a Creator who did not create with pessimistic feelings, but with optimism and joy. Otherwise, how could there be such lavish beauty and diversity in nature? Every living thing testifies to the love of detail. Harmony in creation is an expression of happiness. The feeling of happiness in human beings is connected to harmony in the soul. Without harmony, life cannot exist, but is destroyed. Therefore, the goal of our life should always be happiness, harmony in ourselves and our environment. Whoever is happy wants to pass on happiness. This is a strong expression of love. Happiness and love are mutually dependent. Happiness attracts love and love attracts happiness. Both are expressions of a radiant inner life that is quickly felt by outsiders. People who can hold this feeling and harmony within themselves serve life itself. Professor Gruden:

If the harmony of the universe expects anything from me, it is my inner harmony, so that the absolute harmony is not upset. And the harmony is a feeling of happiness. Accordingly, I came to this world to make my contribution to harmony, that is, to be happy. All the worries, the uncertainty about the realization of my plans, the restlessness because of the events around me disturb me in my service to the all-embracing. So everything just told can be reduced to two words: Be happy![108]

Chapter 5

Perspective of a Scientist

The difficulty is that we naturally like to try to clarify such things by scientific means. And with scientific means that are actually already very outdated. You always think, how does he transfer energy now he is standing at a distance of 10 meters? How can he now transfer energy to this distance, so that my suffering, whatever it is, goes away? But this is just a wrong conception. We must have a completely different picture of nature, a completely different worldview, also a different picture of man. There is not only what natural science describes, what exists in space and time, what our senses perceive, but things that lie beyond that.[109]
Professor Alex Schneider

Life is a big secret — too big. Despite all the discoveries of science, many open questions remain. The rational mind, hungry for knowledge, wishes to penetrate ever deeper into the secrets of life. Past centuries bear witness to great discoveries and new insights. But it seems that many answers raise new questions and the search never ends.

There's More to Life Than Our Senses Can Grasp

It should be clear that there's more to life than our senses can grasp. Even in school we learned that our eyesight and hearing are confined to limited ranges. Even just in physics, we were taught that there are many things that exist but aren't perceived by our senses. A human being can't see 99.999% of the available light (the known electromagnetic spectrum). The part we perceive as visible light is not even the size of a grain of sand compared to the Empire State Building. Research over the last few decades has led to many astonishing findings. In the field of so-called spiritual healing, there are an impressive number of scientific studies that clearly show that this phenomenon is absolutely real. The American psychiatrist Dr. Daniel Benor reviewed and categorized a multitude of studies on the subject of spiritual healing. Significant effects were demonstrated in 76% of the first-class double-blind studies. The evaluation of studies on the topic of remote healing according to the highest scientific standards (Ebneter/Binder) was also able to confirm that it actually works.[110] It was even possible to show that people with special abilities were able to improve the condition of damaged cell cultures and animals. There are relevant publications concerning experiments that prove this beyond any doubt. The leading figure here is the doctor and Harvard professor Gary Schwartz (G. Schwartz, *Energy Healing Experiments*). The American husband-and-wife team Ambrose and Olga Worrall showed in scientifically valid experiments that they were able to act on living organisms at distances of hundreds of kilometers.[111]

The Structure of Matter

Based on the findings of quantum physics and the new atomic model, modern physicists today see the visible world with different eyes. They left the illusion of solid matter behind decades ago. Everything, absolutely everything we see, is made up of atoms. But these atoms, the building blocks of matter, consist of 99.999% emptiness, vacuum, and particle-free physical fields. While there is an atomic nucleus, the ratio in size between the atomic nucleus and the atomic shell is comparable to the ratio of a cherry pit to the roof of Cologne Cathedral. More detailed analysis of the atomic nucleus also reveals a lack of solid matter. The protons and neutrons found in the nucleus consist of even smaller structures, known as quarks. But they can't be isolated, because if you wanted to split a proton into its component parts (three quarks), the energy necessary for this would immediately create new protons. In another model, the elementary particles on which matter is based are seen as vacuum resonances, as so-called nodes of oscillation. In sum, our eyes and external senses everywhere see solid matter, which, if you look at it more closely, consists to the greatest extent of nothing, of emptiness. It would lead us too far afield to examine in detail the latest scientific findings that physically demonstrate that this emptiness that is everywhere, in every atom of our world and in the entire universe, is not empty space. Contrary to popular belief, a physical vacuum is not empty, but rather contains a surprisingly high level of energy, which is referred to as spatial energy. It can even be expressed in numerical terms, although the amount of energy is so high that it is difficult to imagine.[112] Perhaps there is even more still to be found in "empty space" that cannot be measured or calculated today, since there is a lack of understanding and knowledge. What's striking is that we can see parallels on the level of consciousness. Even in silence, in the seeming nothingness, there is an unexpected abundance.

Professor Alex Schneider—the Enigmatic Sides of Nature

Professor Alex Schneider studied high-frequency technology at the renowned research university ETH Zurich. After his studies he worked in industry for several years. He then taught physics at the Kantonsschule St. Gallen for 31 years. Early on, the "enigmatic sides of nature"[113] strongly appealed to him. Inspired by the autobiography of Paramahansa Yogananda, he immersed himself in highly diverse areas of scientific research. He developed into an acclaimed researcher in the area of paranormal science. Since the 1970s, he has given regular interdisciplinary lectures, including at the University of St. Gallen in Switzerland. He endeavored "to make the general public familiar with a too little known aspect of reality."[114] Professor Schneider was co-founder and for 24 years president of the world's leading conference on paranormal science and healing, which was held regularly in Basel (the Basel PSI Days). He has met hundreds of healers and people with special capabilities and examined their abilities. He regularly invited the best of them to his international conference in Basel. Professor Schneider was one of the most skilled and influential experts in the paranormal sciences in the second half of the twentieth century. As with Professor Gruden, I came to know him as a very humorous person with extensive knowledge. I was impressed by his openness to new, inexplicable phenomena. At the same time, he maintained a critical distance and scientific standards as he conducted his examinations. I attended one of his congresses in Basel, where I encountered a broad range of phenomena from many countries. Professor Schneider and his team had invited a wide variety of personalities with exceptional abilities from all over the world. An authentic continuing education was possible at these events. My impression was that phenomena that had previously been given little attention by the established sciences received a serious, open-minded examination here. The congress was very well attended and had several thousand participants representing a healthy mix of medical doctors, psychologists, scientists and interested lay people.

Professor Alex Schneider and His First Encounter with Braco

It was Drago Plečko who made Professor Alex Schneider aware of Braco in the summer of 2005 and gave him some DVDs about Braco. Professor Schneider left the DVDs lying around for a few weeks before he watched them. When he eventually did so, they made a lasting impression.

Drago Plečko sent me videos about Braco. I left them lying around for a long time and then finally watched them. Coincidentally, at that time I had had vexing lower back pain for days that just refused to go away. I could hardly move. And after I watched the videos, it was gone. That startled me quite a bit. I'm usually not someone who reacts so easily to subtle influences.[115]

Manuela Kihm worked closely with Professor Schneider for many years. She directed the largest expo for health and consciousness in Zurich. She describes her first encounter with Braco at an event in Switzerland in 2005:

I observed as unobtrusively as possible the people gathered in the hall, because I wanted to see what would happen to them when they met Braco's gaze. These were very touching moments, because many people present shed tears, some held photos of their loved ones in their hands, and still others were visibly blessed and redeemed. In fact, after meeting Braco, many people present reported their immediate positive experiences on a physical, mental or spiritual level, some with quivering voices and profound words of gratitude. There were also many people who, out of gratitude for their personal recovery or that of a family member or acquaintance, for the renewed love relationship between once quarreling spouses, for the impetus of a new phase of life on an interpersonal or professional level, always come back to Braco.[116]

Braco and Professor Schneider

Together with Professor Schneider, Manuela Kihm traveled to Zagreb at the end of 2005 to experience Braco in his home town. In spring 2006, she invited Braco as a special guest to her "Lebenskraft" expo in Zurich, where he was introduced to hundreds of people by Clemens Kuby. Swiss television reported on the event in its prime-time program. In fall 2006, Braco was an essential part of Professor Schneider's international congress, the Basel PSI Days, which I have previously mentioned. With his characteristic precision and care, Professor Schneider followed what was going on with Braco, beginning in 2005, and spoke with many people who had gone to the events until he resolved to invite Braco to his congress in Basel. Since then, convinced by the extraordinary response to Braco's appearances in Basel and by the experiences congress attendees had with Braco's gift, Professor Schneider has accompanied Braco at events in Germany and Switzerland. He has provided an introduction to thousands of people in the audience and, based on his experience, prepared them for the encounter with Braco's gaze. Professor Schneider decided to summarize his personal experiences and insights in a book. In this work, deeply influenced by his knowledge in physics and his decades of experience in consciousness, spiritual healing and paranormal science, he described and explained Braco and his gift from a scientific point of view in a broadly comprehensible way. His book, *Braco: Die faszinierende Welt von Mythos und Wissenschaft* (English: *Braco: The Fascinating World of Myth and Science*), was published in June 2011.

Braco's Gaze Brings About Profound Harmonization in People

Professor Schneider's goal as a scientist was to more closely approach the "Braco phenomenon," as he called it. Schneider assumes that in whatever way it happens, profound harmonization is brought about in people through Braco. This leads to the people in attendance at the events experiencing externally visible changes in their wellbeing, which he divides into three groups: improvement of people's physical ailments, improvements within their social environment, and long-distance effects. He was particularly impressed by the social changes that manifested themselves as a clearly visible harmonization of interpersonal relationships after attending an event with Braco. In a conversation, he reported examples of estranged married couples and bullying at work. Shortly after attending an event with Braco, a wife found her partner was completely changed. The divorce date had already been set, according to Schneider; but without any apparent external cause, the negative feelings and disharmony had simply dispersed. There was no longer any talk of divorce. Professor Schneider also reported an example related to bullying at work. In this case as well, the strained atmosphere at the office was no longer there after an event with Braco.[117] Professor Schneider:

The social environment of many of those seeking healing is positively influenced in an unexpected and startling way. It might be assumed that the participant returns home with a new and more positive attitude and thus triggers corresponding reactions. But this is certainly not the only reason for a sudden and completely positive change in one's partner, or if there is suddenly a harmonious atmosphere at the office. For most people, however, the occurrence of social changes of this type is completely incomprehensible. These changes can help to re-harmonize our unhealthy environment. To close the circle, there is the incredible effect over vast distances that occurs when participants bring photographs of sick people with them who are thereby liberated from severe suffering. Remember, with Braco, physical healing is the consequence of an inner change that can scarcely be properly discerned. It must consist of a very deep reprogramming of the information that is present in us. An improvement in the basic mental mood, which lasts from hours to weeks, is consistently noticeable in the participants. It's important for feeling a good quality of life, even with physical ailments that haven't healed.[118]

Perhaps you have already experienced a situation where, during a long-distance trip, you thought of your spouse or partner at home, and a short time later your phone rings. Your loved one greets you with the words, "I just had the feeling to call you." The transmission of feelings or thoughts over great distances is a special personal experience. Professor Schneider explains in his book that the existence of telepathy—the transmission of thoughts between people over a distance—has been proven by countless statistically analyzable laboratory experiments. What has been said for telepathy is valid for spiritual healing at a distance, which today is also sufficiently proven.[119]

According to Schneider, what happens with Braco and his gift cannot be explained using a model based on energy transfer or the transmission of any kind of wave over a distance. It's implausible that a beam bearing information originating with a person in Europe could find the targeted person in America. It is more relevant to recognize that on a certain level, we are one with everything. This idea has long been found in the lore of ancient traditions and is today increasingly accepted as a reality. According to Professor Schneider, perhaps one can better understand in this light the extraordinary cases of an encounter with Braco having an effect at a distance. In these cases, participants only have photos of distant people with them, or the social environment of a participant undergoes an inexplicable improvement. Professor Schneider:

With Braco, information that cannot be more precisely described is directly transmitted in the deepest human areas.

This takes place on a level where there is no time. The fact that the group is still gathered for at least a while is simply related to the important fact, which must be repeatedly mentioned, that we need some time to attune ourselves to what is happening. In this state of consciousness, the group is a unit comparable to two people in telepathic contact. Information is not transmitted from one place to another, as we like to imagine in everyday thinking. Some participants experience this unity the first time, others after attending an event with Braco several times. This inner harmony manifests itself, immediately or only after some time, in an external balance, physically, mentally or socially. We have a comparable spaceless state in the many cases involving people suffering far away or a distant social group that experiences improvement through the catalysis of a person attending an event with Braco (and possibly bringing a photograph of the ailing person with them). It must be emphasized that what is presented here is only a model of the metaphysical process. It's certainly more useful than the old scientific view and also more applicable than many esoteric theories, which often try to explain the unknown in a highly inadequate way by using new and nebulous concepts or pseudo-physical terminologies such as vibrations or energies. In the current state of human development, it's time to throw outdated scientific ideas overboard. Our future requires better, more humane worldviews.[120]

Recent findings in physics shed light on a sphere of existence greater than has previously been assumed. In view of the variety of phenomena that are in some ways very difficult to explain, Professor Schneider sees today's physicists as modern esoterics, who, much like mystics hard at work on themselves, find it difficult to interpret the experiences they have had and express them in words. Today's physics needs two fundamentally contradictory models to describe the results of their experiments with light. Light is described as a wave and as a particle at the same time, because in the experiments it shows the properties of a wave at one time, and at another time the properties of a particle. But these models say nothing about what light really is. They only describe two recognizable aspects of light. Light, seemingly such a weak and harmless substance, is actually the greatest force that exists in the universe. It has set the whole creation in motion and brings life. From this point of view, the wave–particle dualism described by physics is only a detail of a much, much bigger picture. Models have to be used to make the incomprehensible more comprehensible. These models describe aspects of a reality that cannot be more firmly grasped. They are neither wrong nor right. There is no absolute truth. The multiple (and in most cases contradictory) models used to describe light illustrate how explanations of even observable phenomena are limited.

Drago Plečko cites a French scientist he met at the international congress in Basel after an event with Braco. He came to a conclusion similar to the one Professor Schneider reached in his book:

A French researcher I met in the corridors of the building where the conference was taking place made an interesting remark that has stuck in my mind. He said: "Provisionally stated, all these people are able to have an effect on different wavelengths and thus affect the various densities of the matter from which people are made, but only the activation of this most subtle level…brings fundamental and enduring changes. And at this conference, we only saw such an effect at the appearance of Braco, the healer from Croatia."[121]

Concepts and explanations are certainly helpful if, as Professor Schneider says, one recognizes the limitations of their explanatory power. Today there is a great deal of literature about the inner life of human beings and the possibilities of the soul's development. It's good to know about it, but the decisive fact is always personal experience. You can write 500 pages on the subject of chocolate without knowing what chocolate really is or how it tastes. You only know that by taking a bite of a chocolate bar.

Chapter 6

Braco and His Predecessor Ivica

The New Age

Today, a fierce awakening is occurring among all of us as an inevitable cry for a more spiritual link of life, for a return to nature, to our hearts and to each other. Our collective consciousness and hearts are calling for help and demanding action to overcome the negative we have done to our natural environment and to our fellow human beings. More and more people are rising to the challenge of correcting inequality before it is too late. We are living in a time of awakening and transformation, which is our present destiny...The limits so easily set by our minds have hindered us until now. Today, our hearts lift such limitations. For our hearts and souls know our most secret desires and hold incorruptibly to the higher understanding that everything is possible, even beyond the comprehension of our minds.[122]
Angelika Whitecliff

In the summer of 2009, the American consciousness researcher and international lecturer Angelika Whitecliff traveled with

Braco for 21 days. She met him for the first time in early 2009 at a paranormal science congress in Nevada, USA. In her book *21 Tage mit Braco* (English: *21 Days with Braco*), she uses the format of a diary to describe her time accompanying Braco. The book is written so vividly that readers have the feeling of being there themselves. In the space of more than 300 pages, she records what she calls "the story of the real man behind the miracles." In three weeks, she was able to discover aspects of Braco that had never been written about before.

Angelika Whitecliff accompanied Braco from early morning to the end of each day, often with only a few hours of sleep because of a demanding itinerary that included events in several European countries. She writes:

> I do not believe that Braco's gift can be transferred to others through learning. And that is because it is a gift to the world from the spiritual source, and only that source can choose the ship that will carry its energy. This is a gift so precious and rare that it cannot be obtained without perfect harmony. If the harmony is lost, this gift also disappears. Therefore, the responsibility is beyond comprehension and must be reflected by the whole soul, and such service is exceedingly rare and precious. To possess such a gift is to serve life itself, without personal interests or thoughts...Fortunately, we do not have to take this burden upon ourselves. The gift is here and is offered to all who are willing to come and experience its effects. It is exclusive and valuable enough to create the transformation we so desire.[123]

In 20 years of travel to many countries on earth, Angelika Whitecliff has never sensed a gift similar to Braco's in any healer or spiritual teacher, as she writes in her book. For her, Braco is manifestly an instrument of a higher power. She emphasizes at one point how important it is to understand that it's not Braco who has a force or power, but rather that a higher force or power has him. He has subordinated his personal life to his gift. Even so, when he appears before groups of people at his events, he doesn't do anything externally. The energy flows naturally out of him in these moments. He just lets it happen.

> His face is always gentle in these moments, and the effect of the power current starts immediately...This intense calm power evoked so much in me, and I knew that many in the group would feel the same power in a variety of ways, within themselves as well as in their lives. I understood completely why so many people keep coming back whenever they can, because the energy can literally recharge the batteries of each individual life in the subtlest and most delicate ways.[124]

In private with his family and friends, Angelika Whitecliff got to know Braco as an ordinary person in every respect. She accompanied him to events in several countries and spent a few days with him and his family on the Adriatic Sea. Braco loves the sea and long walks in nature, and enjoys being with other people. Like any other person, he experiences joy and sadness and can also suffer inside. Angelika Whitecliff was able to observe him in person in many situations, both in private and at events. Her impression was that his personality is characterized by a deep calmness. When interacting with people, he is very generous, patient and compassionate. He has no great ambitions for himself. He loves simplicity and naturalness. He is present and connected to himself in a special way, and he is guided by his spontaneity. It was her impression that he bears an indestructible foundation in his soul that is also accessible to those who look at him. Despite a challenging schedule, he is also always tranquil. Even with all the highs and lows of his life and the momentous task he's been given, he carries within him an extraordinary joy. For Angelika Whitecliff, Braco is the embodiment of a connection to a higher dimension of life. For her, his gift is a gift from God that enables him to receive energy from a higher source and offer it to those who stand in his presence. Over the course of three weeks, Ms. Whitecliff also had very profound personal experiences with Braco's gaze, especially at an event in Skopje, Macedonia.

We all had to be up at 3:30 am to be ready, and packed for the flight back to Zagreb. Everyone had been tired after our dinner, but I was completely energized from my experience... Now I knew with complete certainty my life was governed by something so mysterious and unfathomable, yet loving beyond all comprehension, that I would do anything for this magnificence that I had encountered...After such an occurrence of feeling the true home of consciousness, it was an odd thing to come back into the everyday world...Slowly, and at a pace set by my own spirit, I was rediscovering what people had sought through the ages, and because of Braco, I now saw the assurance of the Golden Age...emerging now for humanity. A gentle, kind man with a youthful spontaneity and enormous spiritual presence, my loving host, the young man from Zagreb, was forging the path.[125]

Angelika Whitecliff

Childhood and Youth

Braco was born on 23 November 1967 at 6:15 a.m. in Zagreb. His parents, Victor and Ivanka Grbavac, named him Josip. His later mentor and friend, Ivica Prokić, gave him the name he goes by today: Braco (Croatian for "little brother"). Braco attended school and university in Zagreb. He had a particularly close relationship with his father. After studying business administration, Braco founded his own company, which enjoyed considerable success. To this day, he has a particular love of nature, especially of water and the sea. Since his early childhood, he has always spent summers on the nearby Adriatic coast, where his parents, like many people in Croatia, have a summer house. He could spend hours alone in the forest or at the seaside. After school or university classes, his friends often found him in Maksimir Park, a large park in Zagreb with five small lakes, forests and landscaped lawns. Braco spent his childhood and youth within his home country, never traveling outside the borders of Croatia. He enjoyed nature and being with his friends and family. He was ordinary in every way. The material goods sought by most people, such as a sports car or the comforts of a prosperous family, were all available to him. Even though on the outside he had everything, during all these years he had a longing for something that he himself couldn't name.

During a lengthy conversation, Drago Plečko asked Braco about his life. Below are a few excerpts. As stated by Braco:

I liked any game that was connected to nature. We always played cowboys and Indians. I was the Indian. I liked playing with a bow and arrow. Later, when I was six or seven years old, I loved fishing and diving in the sea. I was drawn to everything that had to do with water: the sea, the river, the lake. I often rowed a boat. What made me different from my peers was that I liked being alone, especially if I was

around animals or birds. I often went for walks by myself...
At school, my favorite subject was science. Everything that
has to do with nature. Natural history, biology, geography.
I was always drawn to distant lands such as Africa or the
Amazon region, or rivers or Indians. I always watched
shows like that and also travel reports and documentaries.
I dreamed of these countries and wished I could meet the
primitive people there whose lives were so different and
completely connected to nature, not at all like mine. That's
what I dreamed of...I didn't know which path to take. So
later I ended up following the direction of the majority of my
peers. I didn't have any problems in school. I was capable of
more. But I learned it all as a matter of form because I didn't
know what to do with myself...From the outside, everything
looked normal. I never complained. I seemed like a happy
child. A child who actually has everything. But inside, I was
discontented.[126]

In her book *21 Tage mit Braco* (English: *21 Days with Braco*),
Angelika Whitecliff writes about his birth and childhood:

Another warm morning greeted us and as we strolled, Braco
shared his birth story of coming into this world. He was born
premature at seven months, and his mother almost died
in labor. For two months, he was in an incubator and his
mother's milk was placed in a bottle for him. Coming into
the world he only weighed 2.6 pounds (1.3 kilo) and was
18.5 inches (47 cm) long. Next he told me something I had
never heard of before. Braco was born with skin so dark that
he looked like an African parent's newborn, with hair black,
coarse and wavy. The doctors asked his mother afterward if
his father was black, and everyone was very surprised. Soon
after, Braco's skin color became Caucasian like his mother's
and father's; and his hair turned fine, straight and brown.

I could not help but review in my mind all of the ancient tales and prophecies, especially from India, to see if I could remember one in which a special child was born in such a state and later transformed...Another unusual phenomenon of his early years was that until age seven, Braco did not like to eat and he would always throw up his food. Despite this, he was healthy and strong during that time. His childhood would otherwise be normal, and he would spend much occasion in nature. Although he had many friends, he preferred this to playing with the other children all the time. Braco had such a peaceful constancy to him that I asked him, the first time we met, if he was always this way from childhood, or if something had changed him? He answered that he was the same as a child. In the end, I believed his connection with nature, and his love of feeling this connection kept him from filling himself with as many distractions as most other people. I would learn that Braco always had a concrete purity to him and an innocence that was never tainted. His balance was connected with his spontaneity and respect of feelings. These simply conveyed so much more than communication through language, television, books or computers.[127]

Following his father's example, Braco studied business administration in Zagreb. At the age of 24, he successfully completed his studies with a master's degree. Then in 1991/92, to his father's great delight and with his support, Braco founded his own company. But he had to force himself to go to work, even though he was very successful. He knew for a long time that something would happen and that it would completely change his life.

The Encounter with Ivica Prokić

For years, Braco's mother Ivanka suffered from very painful migraines, which doctors could only alleviate but not cure. In

1993, a neighbor told her about an unusual man in Zagreb who helped people without expecting payment. After Ivanka had suffered unbearable pain for months, she decided to follow her neighbor's advice and went to see Ivica on 8 October 1993. Ivica was able to help her. Her pain disappeared. Her son Braco had never been interested in healing or spiritual topics, but he was interested in where his mother had gone. She offered to take him to Ivica. At the time, Ivica Prokić was already established in the building at 1 Srebrnjak Street in Zagreb, the place where Braco's center is to this day. Ivica had rented a small apartment there where he welcomed visitors. That day, 9 October 1993, was the turning point in Braco's life. In a conversation with Drago Plečko, Braco himself spoke of it:

> The decisive moment was when I met Ivica. In that moment I was happy, really happy for the first time. When I first met him and stood in front of him, I felt a kind of inner satisfaction. I left everything I had behind. Without thinking about it, I had ended up where I am today. I had come to someone who was like me. I spent 16 months with Ivica. All I can say is that he had unusual abilities. He could see the past and the future and could help and heal people. The proof is the thousands of people who were helped. At first I couldn't grasp that people would come and he would just touch them and they felt better. He welcomed everyone, regardless of their race or philosophy of life. He was completely natural and spoke just like he thought. He was sort of naturally wild. When I met Ivica, I felt that my search was over. I felt that I had found what I was always looking for in my life.[128]

To the horror of his parents, Braco never returned to working at his company. From one day to the next, he closed that chapter of his life and ever after spent every free minute in the company of Ivica Prokić. Braco observed him going about his work of giving his many visitors the help they longed for. Braco was 26 years old in October 1993 when he first met the person who would later become his mentor and closest friend, and whose successor he would one day become. Ivica had been given special abilities. He knew and saw things that are hidden from everyday consciousness. When Braco first met him, Ivica was able to tell him his most secret thoughts and wishes, which no other person could have known. Braco felt connected to Ivica because they shared the same inner values. No matter how different their external appearances were, they were very similar inside. From the perspective of today, it's clear that Ivica Prokić knew from the start that Braco would be his successor and that Braco would far surpass him in his work. He once told Braco that he wouldn't want to be in Braco's shoes, given what was in store for him. Damir Kambičec, a close associate of Ivica, remembers the day Braco came to Ivica:

That morning, Ivica told me over coffee that someone very special was coming, someone he had been awaiting for a long time. And Braco came with his mother. Ivica told me how beautiful he was, thinking not of Braco's external appearance but of the beauty of spiritual purity…After Braco's arrival, a change appeared in Ivica; he became calm and composed. Previously he was always in a hurry, rushing back and forth. But Braco's arrival brought him peace.[129]

Ivica Prokić

Ivica Prokić

Ivica Prokić was born in the middle of the twentieth century in southern Serbia. Already at the age of seven, he had an initiation experience associated with the sun. His life wasn't easy, considering all that he went through before he came to Zagreb in 1971. Even there, life was a struggle. He often didn't know how he would keep feeding his small family. But he was sustained by the inner certainty that all the hardship he had gone through for decades had a meaning and a purpose. Something would come, some task that would define his future life. He felt a power growing within him that was often expressed through visions. After the first visitors found their way to him and he was able to help them, the number of those seeking aid soon grew. Ivica Prokić felt the pain and suffering of the people around him and an inner calling and strength to help them. Behind Prokić's somewhat coarse façade, love and deep compassion were reflected in his dealings with those seeking help, as visitors report. He was always in a good mood and full of inner strength. He was also very direct and said what he thought. Again and again I learned that Ivica simply knew more; you couldn't fool him. Visitors from that time recount their memories:

> When I first came to see him, he told me some things that no one knew but me. I realized that he had something special in him and that was what drew us all to him. His inner cleanliness and demeanor just drew me to him.[130]

> We talked briefly, he asked a few questions, but right away I felt like he knew everything about me.[130]

> On my first visit, he told me everything I had come to him for.[130]

I had terrible pain in the lower part of my spine and that was the first reason I went to Ivica. When I left the room, my pain stopped. His naturalness and compassion make him stand out from everyone else. He was the first person for whom I felt awe.[130]

A person I don't know, he tells me in a few words everything why I came.[131]

In the few years of his work until his death in 1995, a great many people had come to see Ivica Prokić. He had virtually no personal life. He described his work in a short but expressive phrase: "Giving help." Since January 1993, an apartment in the house at 1 Srebrnjak Street was his place of work; before that, he had spent over two and a half years at 28 Tuškanova Street in Zagreb. Visitors found that improvements in their physical and psychological health, and help with personal life, finances, children, marriage and family, came about miraculously. Prokić evidently had access to knowledge about individual people he wanted to help and a power that could make problems disappear spontaneously, sometimes even suffering that had lasted for years. Otherwise he was, like Braco, a person much like you and me who radiated a zest for life and spoke plainly. Between 1991 and 1995, Ivica Prokić wrote 13 books. Already in his first book, he mentioned that there would be 13 in all. Each book was written in two to three hours without interruption and with no subsequent editing. Each of his books was decorated with a symbol of the sun with 13 rays. He discovered this symbol intuitively and it expresses his work, which was very much focused on the sun as the giver of life. In his books, Ivica Prokić also published letters of thanks. I would like to reprint two examples.

In July 1990, Jagica came to see Ivica. She wrote:

First of all I would like to mention that I had been declared blind, I had to rely on my white cane and didn't see this man at all. When I was guided to him, I was suffering from severe rheumatism.[132]

Ivica refused to help her with her eyes, but she insisted on his continuing to treat her. He would only say that he could try, but he couldn't guarantee that he would be able to help her. Her rheumatic pains decreased, but at first nothing changed with her eyes. Jagica's recollection:

"I was with him on a Friday, and by Monday my condition had improved so much that I no longer needed a cane…I visited Ivica six more times. On a Friday, another miracle happened. When I walked into his office, I saw strange rays of light in my left eye…Then an even greater miracle occurred: As if covered in a thick fog, the figure of a woman appeared to me in the room. I told her there was something shiny on her head—that was her eyeglasses. Then I saw Mr. Ivica. I described his appearance to him and the color of his hair. It's just indescribable how I felt at that moment. All I can do is give thanks. Now I can in fact see and read using my left eye." The mobility problems also disappeared.[132]

Stojanka Dukić visited Ivica Prokić in February 1992. She only went because a colleague had convinced her. She was the manager of a company and, as she put it, had been raised in the spirit of communism. She would never have dreamed of turning to a person like Ivica. But because of her demanding job, she was experiencing burnout. She didn't know how she could go on with her life. Here is an excerpt from her letter:

Nevertheless, with great skepticism, I resolved to visit Mr. Ivica on Tuškanova Street. But then something wonderful began to happen. When I entered the small waiting room there, I immediately felt completely different. There were around ten people in the waiting room. Suddenly a man appeared at the door. I immediately thought, that's a man you don't meet every day...He looked at all of us carefully and then, to my surprise, said my name: "Stojanka, you don't believe in me, so why are you here?" ...He then laughed again and said: "I'll see you. When it's your turn, you'll get what you hope for from this visit." I was let in at about 11 a.m. At the beginning of the conversation he told me that I was the mother of two children. I stared at him. Immediately I was beset by doubt. I didn't contradict him, even though I'm the mother of only one child. He seemed to have read my thoughts: "Yes, Stojanka, you only gave birth to one son, but you also raised a girl since she was a baby after the death of her mother." ...He went on to tell me that I worked at a self-service shop, and that I was the manager there...He also told me that my husband, a former party official, was now retired and did nothing but drink alcohol, which was leading to heated arguments at home.[133]

Ivica Prokić evidently knew details from her life and was even able to foresee future developments. Everything was true. It opened her heart. Ever since the meeting with him, she had felt a great joy in life, and her life had become much easier. Ivica often said goodbye to his visitors by saying: "Go and sing." Few people understood this until they noticed that their pains had disappeared since their meeting with him, or that difficult problems were miraculously resolved or became easier to bear. After a meeting with him, everything somehow changed for the better. Through his work, he created the basis for the development of Braco's worldwide activity today. Once he said about himself:

I am what you are, and you are what I am. I know that your hearts are wounded. I see it, I feel it. What I am is the most dangerous, most powerful and most stubborn path. It's my path.[134]

The Trip to South Africa and the Death of Ivica Prokić

Braco was able to spend 16 months at the side of Ivica Prokić. He wasn't only with him throughout his work in Zagreb, but also accompanied him on his trips to Germany. There they met groups of people in several cities who were hoping for help from Ivica. On a trip to Germany in February 1995, a South African named Nenad came to see Ivica Prokić in a town near Stuttgart. Nenad had already been there a few weeks earlier and now was coming for the second time. Since his last meeting with Ivica, his advanced-stage cancer had improved significantly. Braco describes this meeting in his book *Nach der großen Tragödie* (English: *After the Great Tragedy*):

Nenad said: "I had cancer and visited numerous doctors in Germany, South Africa and Switzerland. All of them always said the same thing at the end: We can't promise you anything. I spent a lot of money on it, around 30,000 German marks." Then Ivica asked: "And how much did you pay me?" "Nothing to you, sir. I bought your book and paid for it. But that's normal, because you also have costs…I don't know who you are in reality. But after I was with you, the doctors said at the check-up that my disease had disappeared. They could hardly believe it themselves. I've never believed in bioenergetics, prophets or supernatural powers, but this here is reality. After I visited Ivica, my disease disappeared.[135]

Out of gratitude, this man invited Ivica and his companions to vacation in South Africa. Ivica had never taken a vacation. He found it very difficult to agree to the trip, as he sensed that something would happen there, but his special love for the people of sub-Saharan Africa was well known. Eventually, he decided to make the flight after all. On 16 April 1995, he flew to Durban with his six closest associates. Braco's mother, Ivanka Grbavac, recalls the event:

> Before going to Africa [where Ivica died], I told Ivica the night before not to go because I felt something would happen. He said that now everything was finished and he must go.[136]

In Durban, Ivica didn't mind driving 200 kilometers to a beach near St. Lucia to swim there. A large wave cost Ivica his life at 11 a.m. on 23 April 1995. He drowned on the coast of the Indian Ocean. Ivica wrote 13 books. He titled the last book *Novi Pocetak* (English: *New Beginning*). At the end of the book, he writes:

> *Ja sam vidio trinaest mojih knjiga, proročanstvo se i ovo doista obistinilo, radio sam i uradio, pisao i napisao, sada završavam i mnogo vam sreće želim. Kraj*

I have seen thirteen of my books. The prophecy really came true. I have worked and labored, composed and written. Now I'm done and I wish you good luck. The End

Chapter 7

A New Beginning

Congress Würzburg, Germany, 2019

Braco never expected to continue Ivica Prokić's work. He couldn't believe that he too would be able to help people as Ivica had. Ivica's sudden death deeply affected him. When he returned, hundreds of people were waiting at the airport, and for the first three days he had to keep telling despairing visitors what had happened in South Africa. On 8 May 1995, he started his work in the same place as Ivica before him: in the building at 1 Srebrnjak Street in Zagreb. He had often been told that he too could do what Ivica had done, but he vehemently rejected the idea. It was the most difficult time in his life.

A few days after returning from South Africa, a middle-aged woman came to Braco at 1 Srebrnjak and asked him to touch her daughter's picture in order to help her. In a conversation with Drago Plečko, Braco described what happened:

Finally, on the third day, a woman came to me after my speech as everyone was leaving. She asked me if I could help her. I said I hadn't done that before and didn't see how I could help her. She asked me to touch a photo of her child, who was plagued by nightmares. She believed that my touch would help her child. I obliged her, and after three days she returned with a bouquet of flowers. She thanked me warmly and said that her child was doing better, that the nightmares had disappeared. So I started my work spontaneously.[137]

Now there was no hiding the fact that Braco also had a special gift for helping people. The number of people who came to ask for help kept increasing. The building at 1 Srebrnjak, a street in an attractive part of Zagreb, was the place where Ivica Prokić had laid the foundation for the work that he always referred to as "giving help." Now it was Braco continuing his work.

Thousands Are Coming

In this world, there is nothing to which we can adhere and nothing that is completely certain. That is why everyone should follow his inner voice, or, as some say, the voice of his heart. Those who come to me need not think about it, for I do not ask them to renounce their faith or anything else. About many I know next to nothing. But they return again and again and persistently claim that they are being helped.[138]

I believe that the goal is to achieve complete freedom, which will then allow people to surrender themselves to intuition, which will safely lead them to what is best for them. Not necessarily what is most pleasant, but what is best. For that matter, setting this process in motion in all of these people is also my mission.[139]
Braco in conversation with Drago Plečko

Braco belongs to a rare group of gifted people who do not rely on the authority of sacred scriptures or deities. He is open to all people regardless of their nationality, religion or education.

At first, Braco still spoke to visitors, touched photos and signed books in order to provide help. Every day, he was in Zagreb in the house at 1 Srebrnjak where his predecessor Ivica Prokić had started in 1993. Visitors were able to come freely. However, from year to year more and more people came and brought their life dramas and problems to Braco in the hope of help. Braco often traveled to Germany on weekends when he was invited to events. Wherever he went, people were waiting for him. Some had chartered buses to get there. It was not uncommon for him to work for 13 hours after a long drive to Germany, only to spend another 12 hours the next day receiving visitors one at a time in another city. At the end of this was the 10-hour drive back to Croatia. When people came to see him in Zagreb, he was there for them every day during the week except Thursdays. But Braco, as he once expressed in a conversation, feels no fatigue no matter how long he works. Since the beginning of his work in May 1995, Thursday has been Braco's day of rest, his day off during the week. Ivica had chosen Thursday as the rest day for himself, and Braco followed his example. What started in this simple way continued later, even when traveling by air due to tight deadlines and invitations to events on four continents. To this day, the events are prepared and conducted by the people and organizations who have invited Braco.

In the same way that Braco's activity and his work have nothing to do with a medical or healing activity, they are also in no way connected with institutionalized religion, which Braco respects just as much as he does medicine. When asked by Drago Plečko how he feels about religious believers or clerics who criticize his work, Braco replied:

If we want to know the truth about ourselves, we have to look inside ourselves and not focus on other people and their work. The truth is not what appears to us to be truth, but mostly something completely different. I wish good luck and happiness to everybody equally, both to those who criticize me and those who love me.[140]

In 2002 Braco flew to Israel for the first time. Isaac, the owner of a company, had invited him and organized several events for his employees and their relatives and friends. In 2004, Braco was welcomed by 7600 people in one place in Bosnia. After more than 36 hours of working one on one with people, it was obvious that his approach had to change. Since that day, people attending events with Braco come only in groups, and he offers them his gaze. Also since that time, he has not spoken in public. Invitations to major conferences followed, such as the 2006 conference for consciousness and healing in Basel that I described in detail above. Through this conference, the media in Germany, Austria and Switzerland became aware of Braco, and there were more and more invitations to events in various European countries. The overview below highlights only a few prominent events during the following years. ORF, the Austrian national broadcaster, helped make Braco known throughout Austria on its *Primavera* primetime show in January 2007. The show triggered a large surge of people from Austria and neighboring countries who came to see Braco. Many came to the events held in several Austrian cities. As in previous years, on Braco's fortieth birthday, 23 November 2007, thousands of people bearing flowers came from countries in Europe and abroad. This has been repeated each year up to the present day.

In April 2008, Braco was invited to Italy for the first time. In Bellaria near Rimini, an international conference on the paranormal sciences was held each spring. Here, too, Braco was met by auditoriums full of guests. In fall 2008, over 5000 people attended an event with Braco in Budapest. Later that year, there were 10,000 in attendance in Skopje, Macedonia. An international journalist, Paola Harris, who had heard about Braco in Rimini, wanted to introduce him to the American public. In February 2009, this led to an invitation to an international conference in Laughlin, Nevada. Before his return to Europe, Braco was invited to a number of cities in the continental USA and Hawaii. As mentioned above, he visited the USA frequently over the next few years, and also traveled to Japan, Australia and Indonesia, and later to Mexico and the Dominican Republic. In 2013 and following years, he was invited to offer his gaze in various cities in Russia. The director of a large company organized the events because he had experienced Braco's gaze in Zagreb himself and was very impressed. He wanted to make this opportunity for help available to his compatriots free of charge. He rented rooms, printed books and even paid for buses to bring people to the event locations from the surrounding areas at his own expense. So many people came that sometimes the hall was too small and events were held outdoors.

As in the USA, film teams documented the visitors' experiences at these events. Furthermore, Braco traveled to England, Ireland, Portugal, Spain, Denmark, Finland, the Czech Republic, Belgium, Slovenia, Romania, Slovakia and the Netherlands. Until the COVID-related lockdown in March 2020, Braco continued to attend events in various countries almost every weekend and in some cases for nearly an entire week at a time, as the local organizers asked for repeat visits. Planned trips to other countries had to be postponed due to the pandemic. Instead, Braco began offering free online events almost daily via live streaming in March 2020. These events brought together people from around 70 countries.

At events with Braco, a striking feature is that most guests bring flowers with them. If they go into the session with Braco, the bouquet will be handed in beforehand. On leaving the room after the session, everyone is given back a different bunch of flowers. This practice arose purely by chance and has persisted over the years. Many of the visitors bring flowers as a sign of respect, while others bring them out of gratitude. Others simply feel the need to express their feelings through the flowers when they come to see Braco. The flowers are an expression of their joy and love for the person who has helped them so much in life. By receiving different flowers at the end, they take something with them that reminds them of the encounter with Braco and connects them to it through their feelings. So the flowers they take home with them have a special meaning.

International Peace Award, United Nations, New York, 2012

On 16 November 2012, Braco was invited to New York by a UN organization. There he was awarded an international peace prize, the Peace Pole. The Dalai Lama, Mother Teresa and Pope John Paul II had previously received this award. At the presentation of the peace prize in the Tillmann Chapel at the United Nations, Rev. Deborah Moldow said:

It is time to build a new culture of peace and that is where Braco comes in. I feel that that is exactly what Braco brings through his gazing, he gives each person a personal experience of peace…The Peace Pole that we gave Braco at the UN—that was such a special moment. It was not only awarding him the Peace Pole but also allowing the people from the United Nations community who had gathered there

to appreciate Braco as an "Ambassador of Peace"...[141]
In a conversation with Drago Plečko, Braco commented on his tireless, decades-long activity:

> I can only say that I'm happy. I believe there is no greater happiness or satisfaction than when you can help someone or do good. I'm really satisfied with it. Helping people is my greatest prize. An indescribable feeling of satisfaction and happiness.[142]

Live Streaming

The first time I saw Braco over live streaming, in October last year, I said to myself, just try it out and see what happens. The three of us were standing in front of the computer and suddenly I felt this huge wave of energy coming through and I thought, oh my god, this is really real.[143]
A visitor from the USA

It started with a Skype session between Zagreb and Hawaii initiated in November 2009 by Angelika Whitecliff, the author of the book *21 Days with Braco*. To everyone's great surprise, the participants in the small group that Ms. Whitecliff had called together felt a strong energy in their bodies. Many couldn't hold back their tears, while others felt a clear sense of spiritual relief. The reactions were just like those at the live events with Braco. This was the beginning of regular online broadcasts of Braco's gaze, which were perfected over time through the growing possibilities of technology. Sometime later there was to be an event with Braco at Mount Shasta in California. However, he could not travel to the event because his visa was not available in time. For this reason, the first live-stream transmission of Braco's gaze was organized from Germany. The camera in the studio in Germany transmitted his gaze via the Internet to the hall in the USA. The American film team documented the exciting experience of one visitor:

> The first time I saw Braco was at Mount Shasta. He wasn't there in person. I didn't know what to expect and I had concerns about the five-hour drive. It really hurts when you have sciatica and have to sit in a car. It was painful. And so I was a little scared about driving for five hours, not experiencing any healing, and then driving back in even more pain. I was in terrible pain. I would wake up at night, crying in pain and asking for mercy. I saw Braco at the event only through live streaming and I've had no pain ever since. I didn't feel anything during the session, but it was gone the next morning. I feel like a living miracle.[144]

Later the live streaming was organized by two teams, one from the USA and one from Europe, and the technology was expanded over time. In the beginning, there was a small fee for viewers to cover expenses. In May 2014, a team in Russia organized free live streaming with Braco. Any costs incurred were covered by a sponsor in the country. Soon after, many viewers from Europe also wanted to support European live streaming. Since then, the live stream with Braco has been accessible to everyone free of charge (www.braco-tv.me). In the years that followed, Braco's gaze was streamed live once each month. This has been changed to almost daily broadcasts since March 2020 due to the pandemic. The sessions with Braco are transmitted worldwide from his center at 1 Srebrnjak in Zagreb. Below are comments from two participants:

> For more than 20 years, I've suffered from pain as a result of an accident. I was very skeptical about whether the live streaming with Braco and his gaze could help me. When I heard about Braco, I thought, *That's just one more healer,*

but there was something that attracted me. So I told myself, *I have nothing to lose. I'll just watch this person in the online broadcast.* I felt a powerful energy and my body felt very hot. When I saw him on screen, only one thing came out of me: "Please help me." Then I felt the heat in my body getting stronger and stronger, and then all the pain was just gone. It just happened within seconds. The next day I worked in the garden for hours, but the pain I had had for so many years never came back.[145]

I participated in two online sessions. At the beginning I was very skeptical, but in the first session I felt totally calm, which is very unusual for me. But mostly I felt like someone was taking a great burden from me. When I left, I felt a joy and ease that I hadn't felt for a long, long time.[146]

The Voice

When Braco began to travel to other countries, he looked for a solution so that those who continued to come to Zagreb to see him could receive what his gaze imparts, but in another way. He wrote a text, went to the recording studio and read the words aloud, resulting in an approximately 10-minute recording. This recording of his voice was played for the people who had come to see him. Just by listening to his voice, they experienced the same physical and mental improvements and the same change in their consciousness that others experienced from his gaze. People reacted very positively. When listening to the recording of Braco's voice, just as when experiencing his gaze, a definite sense of energy is perceptible in the body. It's not even necessary to understand the content of the words spoken in Croatian. I have been able to observe this several times at events in German-speaking countries where Braco was not personally present. Imagine hearing a text in a foreign language and not understanding a word, and yet something touches you, you feel strengthened inside, so that you want to hear this recording again and again. Many scientists have sought answers for this remarkable phenomenon. Voice analyses were carried out to look for particular frequencies. These frequencies were detected, and yet the effect of Braco's voice cannot only be derived from measurable frequencies. As with his gaze, what is there through his voice can also only be experienced personally. That is why I would like to let some visitors speak again at the end of this chapter. They tell about their experiences at 1 Srebrnjak Street, Zagreb, after listening to Braco's voice:

> For me, it's unimportant whether Braco is physically present or whether I hear his voice. I feel the energy flowing through my body. Sometimes in my tears, which aren't actually important. I'm satisfied and happy. I thank him with all my heart for everything.[147]

> Braco's voice means a lot to me. Inside, I'm really moved. I feel like something completely pure and clean is entering into me. I can say that it's something wonderful. I feel a change in me, in myself. I've started to appreciate the real, true values in life. I knew nothing about them before. I've seen the same change in many other people.[147]
> (A young woman from Croatia)

> I feel warmth, a strong energy, as if something relieves me. Through his voice, my sister was helped. I had a picture of her with me.[147]

Mr. Simon, an Austrian, sought help for his wife Nada, who was in a wheelchair after suffering a brain hemorrhage 17 years earlier. She could neither walk nor speak. During his visit to 1 Srebrnjak in Zagreb, however, he did not meet Braco in person. Only Braco's voice was played. As Mr. Simon reported in an interview on camera, he went to the encounter with Braco's voice with only a photo of his wife. Two days later, his wife was able to speak again and walk 10 meters without crutches. The attending physician at the hospital commented:

> I can't explain it in terms of conventional medicine. She has never been able to walk freely and now suddenly she is walking. And the talking is really fascinating to me.[148]

Miranda, a dental colleague of mine, shared a personal experience with the voice of Braco with me. She went to Zagreb to attend an event with Braco. But he was away traveling. So she went to an event with his voice. Her mother had suffered from pain in her right arm for months. Despite medical therapy, she could hardly move her arm. Her mother was very sad and unhappy about this situation. She did not know that her daughter was going to an encounter with Braco to ask for help in her heart. Miranda:

> Before the recording of Braco's voice started during the event, I only thought about my mother and wished that she could smile and be happy again. When I came back to Split two days later, my mother smiled and she joyfully told me: "I have no pain at all anymore!" She was very happy and could move her arm freely again. It never came back.[149]

Chapter 8

The Sun Symbol — a Symbol of Great Significance

Sun Symbol in Onyx Room in Braco's Center at 1 Srebrnjak
Street, Zagreb

The symbol of the sun with the 13 rays is not the symbol of the sun in the sky, but the sun inside us that illuminates your life from within and will bring you joy and happiness, no matter if you drive a Rolls Royce or an old jalopy, no matter if you look to the future with hope or with fear.[150]
Braco in conversation with Drago Plečko

"It Is the Strongest Symbol I Have Seen So Far" (Plečko)

On the cover of every book and DVD by Braco and his predecessor Ivica, there is a symbol of the sun with 13 rays. Ivica Prokić discovered this symbol through intuition. It held great significance for him as an external expression of his work.

'n the past, a symbol of the sun has been found among many vilizations, as the sun is clearly the dispenser and guarantor of all life on earth. The sun symbol that expresses the work of Braco and his predecessor Ivica is a sun with 13 rays. There is no doubt that there is something more about this symbol. It seems to express something special. People who wear it as a piece of jewelry have described "a feeling of connection to a special place in my heart,"[151] or "a connection to the power within me."[151] They claim that they feel a lot of strength from this symbol, and protection. Some felt immediately attracted when they saw it for the first time: "When I saw the sun symbol at my friends' house, I knew that I had to come here."[151] Symbols have accompanied people for a long time and usually have a personal meaning for the wearer. They always express something that we cannot or do not want to express in words. They mostly have an individual, personal value. So the fact that Braco and his predecessor Ivica value the symbol of the sun with 13 rays highly aroused my special interest in Braco's sun symbol.

Rudina, a colleague of mine, told me that she had dreamt of this very symbol two decades before she first learned about Braco. In a dream, she saw it with its 13 rays, which are attached in a very specific way. Some dreams are quickly forgotten, but she couldn't forget this particular dream. She had been looking for this symbol ever since. It had touched something inside her. When she heard about Braco and saw his sun symbol, she knew that it was the precise symbol from her dream. Drago Plečko, the most important Croatian authority in the field of consciousness and paranormal sciences, attributed great significance to this symbol. From his point of view, it is the most powerful symbol he has encountered on his travels to meet the leading spiritual figures of East and West. Drago Plečko:

I've always been curious about the meaning of Braco's special fondness for the symbol of the sun with thirteen rays, which has an extraordinarily powerful effect on those around him, even if from an objective point of view they don't know what it actually represents. Symbols that make an impact must have a special meaning in order to unite in the human consciousness all these opposites and inconsistencies that accompany human beings to the ends of their lives. This concept, the desire for the creation of a possibility of salvation, or of a savior himself, has always been called the "filius solis et lunae," "son of the sun and moon," or the harmony of ying and yang. The sun is clearly symbolized by its physical appearance and the moon by the number of rays—thirteen—which, as we have already established, represent the thirteen months of the lunar year, that is, the energy of the moon, which according to some schools of thought reflects the processes that take place in the unconscious part of our personality. It's remarkable how Ivica Prokić, Braco's predecessor and a simple man, intuitively created such a strong symbol of something that the brightest minds of twentieth-century psychoanalysis argue about. The affinity of so many people for this symbol in particular testifies to its archetypal power.[152]

After a 2019 event with Braco in Marchtrenk, Austria, I met a young woman who wanted to share a story about her son. Weeks before, she had bought a small pendant with the sun symbol for her son. It was a spontaneous feeling that she wanted to give her son a gift. The 14-year-old knew little about Braco and did not have a great interest in his mother's preferences. However, he liked the gold pendant and was happy to wear it. Not long afterwards, the following occurred:

After a few weeks, my son asked me what I had given him. Since he had been wearing this pendant, he had the feeling that everything in and around him had become brighter; it was as if a fog was receding.[153]

In another case, a woman reported that she had received two small ear studs in the shape of the 13-pointed sun from her daughter. She put them on, and a few minutes later her tinnitus (ringing in the ear) that had persisted for more than two years disappeared. The tinnitus had been so severe that she had to go out onto the street at night because silence made the ringing intolerable.[154] I also learned from another woman that the nightmares from which she had suffered for over 40 years disappeared on the same day that she hung the pendant in the shape of the sun symbol around her neck. Since then, she has never had another nightmare — after 40 years![155]

Braco's Dream

A few days after his first meeting with Ivica Prokić in October 1993, Braco had a dream. Moved by this dream, he went to a goldsmith and had a golden pendant made in the shape of the sun symbol that he saw on Ivica's books. In gratitude, he gave the pendant to Ivica. Professor Alex Schneider describes this encounter in his book in detail:

> After visiting this mysterious man, who deeply impressed him, for about two weeks, Braco wanted to make him happy by surprising him with a gift. He remembered a dream in which a sun with thirteen rays had appeared to him. Braco considered this sun a symbol of Ivica's work.
>
> He took a pencil and drew a detailed picture of the sun on a sheet of paper. With this sketch Braco went to a goldsmith, had a golden pendant made with a diameter of about five centimeters and had it attached to a massive gold necklace. Timidly and uncertainly, Braco put the present on Ivica's desk, then left immediately so that Ivica would have no opportunity to turn down the gift. The next morning Braco came to Ivica with trembling knees. He was uncertain whether his gift would be properly understood and accepted.

As he walked up to Ivica he had an uneasy feeling. "My boy," said Ivica in a calm voice, "I have seen your present. My first thought was to give it back to you right away. I know that you had the best intentions with it, and I also know that it is really very expensive. But you must know that money and wealth haven't the slightest importance in my life."

Then Ivica looked at Braco with a grim glance and asked, "Do you know where that necklace is now?" "I don't know," answered Braco. "You'll probably give it back to me now." "If my inner voice had not ordered me to accept this present, I would have given it back to you in any case. But in this case...", with a slight grin on his face, Ivica slowly opened his shirt, from where the first golden rays of light from Braco's necklace flashed forth. "But in this case," Ivica went on, "I have no other choice. I will wear this necklace!" Braco was satisfied. But for Ivica, the matter was not yet dealt with. It was October 1993 when Ivica received the gift. He turned to Braco and said, "For your birthday next month you'll be getting exactly the same chain from me. Just the two of us will then wear these necklaces!" A few months later especially the people close around Ivica received a smaller version of the sun pendant.[156]

The symbol of the 13-rayed sun is also closely connected with the metal gold. Gold has had a special meaning as a solar metal for a long time in many cultures. It is said to symbolize the sun but also the heart. Some attribute to it specific, even spiritual properties that are not found in other metals. The golden sun with 13 rays is considered the visible expression of the work of Ivica and Braco; it is the symbol of their gift.

Chapter 9

Statements by Doctors and Psychologists

Professor Jasminka Peršec, Medical Doctor, Specialist in Anesthesia, Croatia

The phenomenon of Braco's gaze goes back to the 1990s when Braco, as a young economist searching for himself or for a higher purpose of existence, encountered Mr. Ivica at 1 Srebrnjak. At the time, the small modest office in which Mr. Ivica worked was not even as big as the room where Braco now works. There are two important things to emphasize here: first, time flies, and in the many years that have passed, interest in the help Braco offers hasn't ceased. It has instead increased sharply with the number of people who follow his work. And second, simplicity, durability and accessibility have been characteristic features of both Ivica and Braco throughout the course of their lives and work. Braco's popularity hasn't changed him or made him less accessible and generous, which is typically the case with popular public figures. The manner of communication in the everyday world today teaches us that it's imperative to say something clever but moderate, and we spend a lot of time communicating and analyzing communication. And even now, in the current situation of a global pandemic, we're witnessing the production of an immense amount of information that exhausts individuals who are trying as best they can to understand, accept, and help themselves. But this isn't so easy, because in the sea of information, how can we know what's acceptable and necessary, and what will provide help and solutions? So we can spend hours and days analyzing and trying to explain a problem or situation without being even in the general vicinity of a solution. Our civilization has now reached the point where it's better to be silent than to create a stir by saying too much. What Braco provides with ease through his eyes is liberating and brings peace and calmness, just as the sun can warm us as we sit on the terrace or in nature and absorb its warmth, or the rustling of the wind in the forest or the birds in the trees...So simple, so mundane, so small, and yet so immensely full. The Braco phenomenon can be analyzed, or simply accepted as a breath of positive energy, and you can use it for yourself.

There are no simple equations in medicine, and we're frequently unable to fully predict the progress of a treatment or operation, even though we've performed it exactly according to professional standards. It often comes as a surprise to us when someone who, by all medical criteria, has a lower chance of recovery ultimately gets well (even becoming healthier than someone who should be easy to treat), and we can't attribute it to our technique because we did the same thing, we used the same treatment or surgery. What constitutes this "bonus plus" for each person is the power of positive thinking. Braco radiates this positive energy just by looking at you. There are no words to make noise and disturb the peace. This positive energy is really able to do anything for us, but only if we let it. It appears that Braco can bring about significant progress in an individual's life, but this desire, the individual's own choice and openness, is the key to success. Finally, it's important to say that Braco doesn't ask for anything. He's simply there for everyone who is seeking and desiring and wants to change themselves. The energy of love and friendliness does no harm to anyone, and the one who receives it can only benefit from it and make significant progress in their personal life in today's turbulent daily routine.

Lucia de Leon Colizoli, Medical Doctor, Specialist in Psychiatry, USA

It's an honor and a pleasure to join the many other doctors worldwide who are able to appreciate the profound impact of Braco's work on those who participate in his events in person and through live streaming. Since January 2011, I've seen Braco in person on numerous occasions in four cities in the USA and three European cities, and I've participated in live streaming events online. Braco's effect on me and others was profound and created a feeling of happiness, optimism, vitality, compassion, and a sense of oneness with others and the world that I've never known anywhere else despite having had extensive contact with groups focused on expanding consciousness. I will try to describe some of what I've observed. There are very moving incidents of health improvement, even in cases of severe illness.

A 17-year-old boy was diagnosed with sarcoma and told his leg would have to be amputated immediately. He didn't know about Braco, but his aunt and her friends brought the boy's picture with them to events with Braco for five days. Immediately afterward, his diagnosis was downgraded and an amputation was no longer required. The boy fully recovered.

A woman had a tumor in her breast that was confirmed by radiology. The tumor disappeared after an event with Braco. It was possible to confirm this at a medical checkup. The woman hadn't received any further medical treatment.

Numerous people with chronic depression and/or anxiety have reported a lasting disappearance of symptoms after attending an event with Braco. A man I met at an event in New York spoke of his deep grief and severe depression because of a death in his family. The grief disappeared and his mood stabilized after an event with Braco. I interacted with him personally. As a doctor, I've never seen such dramatic improvement so quickly.

I've observed numerous young people with a history of very poor school grades, poor comprehension and/or inattentiveness who show dramatic improvement after attending an event with Braco, even graduating from college later. These students were not treated by doctors.

A nurse with a large fibroid tumor in her uterus was scheduled to undergo an operation. After seeing Braco, her surgeon examined her again and found that the tumor had disappeared.

People have reported that lifelong allergies or asthma have disappeared after attending an event with Braco, and in one case, after hearing a recording of his voice. These improvements were long lasting.

A man with impairment following a heart attack reported complete and sudden relief from these symptoms after attending an event with Braco. The man had initially been skeptical of Braco.

It's not unusual to hear reports of spontaneous and lasting remission from alcohol and drug addiction. A Vietnam War veteran with decades of post-traumatic stress symptoms—insomnia, fear of attack, flashbacks, depression—reported a complete recovery from these symptoms after his experience with Braco's gaze. Other people with PTSD have reported similar improvements.

A woman in her seventies with chronic pain who needed a cane to walk and had had difficulty breathing for years after a car accident reported immediate and dramatic improvement after an event with Braco. The improvements were confirmed by the physician treating her.

A young woman around 30 years old was looking for an old friend, but had no current address or phone number, just his inactive Facebook page. Immediately after an event with Braco, he replied to her on Facebook. They married a year later and are now happy, with one baby and a second on the way.

After seeing Braco, many family members have suddenly gotten back together after years of separation.

There are many reports of these types of transformations that cannot be simply dismissed as mere coincidence. This presence, this "vibration" that Braco shares so freely, is urgently needed in the world today. All of us in the medical professions can benefit from it in our own work. In these times of climate crisis and global pandemic, Braco's almost daily live streaming events connecting thousands around the world in an intense web of joy and peace are a great help to people.

Dirk Leijten, Physician, Netherlands

A few years ago, a colleague asked me to record testimonials from people attending events with Braco in Amsterdam. Until then, I hadn't really known anything about this man from Croatia. It was remarkable to see how enthusiastic and passionate people were to tell me about their experiences with Braco. I also noticed that later when I was watching the various DVDs about Braco. Very remarkable. One of the first testimonials is still very clear in my mind to this day. A woman from London—she had flown to Amsterdam specifically to meet Braco—had suffered from low back pain for years, but recovered completely during a session with Braco. She spontaneously demonstrated to me how she could move her back in all directions without any restriction. Her husband joyously confirmed her story. One man told of prolonged shoulder pain that completely disappeared even before he attended the session with Braco. He was waiting to be admitted to the auditorium of the hotel in Amsterdam where Braco was offering his gaze. He was scheduled to be in the next group. But all the pain had already disappeared. What I notice again and again about the live meetings with Braco is that the group of people present gives me the feeling that everyone is at home, everyone counts, everyone is seen. It feels familiar, safe and powerful in a positive way. I have attended events with Braco myself. During those moments, the emotional, visual and physical sensations I experience are hardly remarkable. However, I always feel very happy and in a good mood when I'm on my way to or returning from a meeting. These are all moments when I feel freed from the pointless aspects of life that cost so much useless energy and attention, and when I feel connected to what really matters in life: gratitude. This became clear to me during a meeting in Visoko, Bosnia. Tears were running down my cheeks out of pure gratitude. I had gotten past a difficult phase in my life quite well and had come out of it more quickly, better and stronger than I would have ever thought possible.

I can testify like no one else that what is working through Braco is very powerful. A 34-year relationship had definitively come to an end. I was open to a new relationship. At a live meeting in Amsterdam, I had expressed my desire for "the best woman for me" during the session—only in my thoughts. A short time later I met this woman, who I'm very happy with.

Finally, I'd like to report on my experience with the sun symbol. Since time immemorial, people have surrounded themselves with symbols of strength, luck and protection. Except for a wedding ring, I've never worn jewelry with a symbolic meaning. For several years now, I've been wearing the sun symbol on a necklace and a ring. When I have to take the ring off due to my job as a doctor, I place it near me. And it feels good. Especially when I consciously focus, they give me a feeling of inner peace and the confidence that everything will be fine. Not only for me, but also for the people around me.

How does Braco manage to do this? As already mentioned, what's important is not the answer to this question, but rather the realization, as I have repeatedly observed, that people evidently experience help in a wide variety of areas through the encounter with Braco. The experiences of the people I spoke to at the events with Braco in Amsterdam are quite remarkable. From a medical point of view, I can't explain the improvements to health and in various other areas of life. That can't be ignored.

Simona Zdravkov, Medical Doctor, Italy

It's difficult to express my feelings about this person, who really means a lot to me. My life changed through the encounters with Braco and his gaze. I was helped in this way to become what I am today. I'm a doctor and currently work in Italy, although originally I'm from Macedonia. I grew up in a very small town in Macedonia in what is, let's say, a "dysfunctional" family. A lot of arguments, a lot of secrets, a lot of judging... We lived in a house with my father's parents and his brother. We were poor and my parents barely made it to the end of each month, but my sister and I always had everything we needed. One day in 2003 my father lost his job and decided to come here to Italy. It was hard, especially for him, but we had to stay strong. A lot of things went wrong in my early life. One trauma I experienced was being sexually abused by my cousin for four years. I was angry at the world and I couldn't stand anyone. Worse still, I had Stockholm Syndrome (where the victim falls in love with the perpetrator). I was full of hate and full of questions that no one could answer. Until one day in 2007, when my aunt and uncle told us about Braco. I found the strength to end the abuse. I was able to process everything that had happened without the aid of psychiatrists. From my point of view, that's the most surprising thing, because this power that comes through the eyes of Braco is able to reach the deepest and innermost layers in people. Every time I come to events with Braco and his quiet gaze, I feel as if I'm standing in front of a large waterfall of light. I feel something so powerful hugging the people in the room and lifting them out of their misery like a phoenix. Because that's what happened to me. I was like trash, dead inside, and I rose up like a phoenix does. That was my victory.

My professional life has also been affected. After graduating in Macedonia, I moved to Italy in 2015. Everyone told me it would be impossible to become a doctor here. First I had to learn the language (not easy at all!), then I had to find a way to have my diploma recognized. I enrolled at a university here in Italy again and they told me I had to pass seven exams and then write my doctoral dissertation. Whether you believe it or not, I was able to do it all in about six months! I'm not a genius, I'm not a very clever person, but through Braco and his gaze I had gained a special connection, a power that helped me to achieve what had seemed impossible to me. Another thing I've learned is patience. For every single thing in life, you just need patience. Everything comes at the right time. Don't make plans; accept whatever comes, whether good or bad. I waited and found a job two months after receiving my license. I'm still there, at an emergency medical center near Milan. Working with people isn't easy. Different characters, different culture...Once again, thanks to Braco and his energy, I'm able to cope with the stress and difficulties associated with this type of work. The days at work following events with Braco are amazing. I'm able to see and empathize with people differently and just understand the patients I meet more deeply. I have a different calmness and peace in me. When I go out into the waiting room to call for patients who may have been waiting there for hours, they don't yell at me like they do at others. At first I thought it was strange, but then I realized that there was something inside me that I'd gotten ever since I started attending the events with Braco. It also often helps me arrive at the right answers and diagnoses. During COVID, the only thing that kept me sane was Braco's sun symbol that I wear. With the number of hours I worked, I thought I would need months of rest, but no. I was able to accept every challenge and overcome every fear.

You can't describe Braco and his miracles. You simply have to experience them. I can only say: thanks for everything I've been given since I found Braco and his silent gaze.

Oliver Bonifer, Physician, Specialist in Gynecology, Austria

My experience with a special person
In summer 2015, I attended an event with Braco in Berlin. It was 13 September 2015 when I entered the convention center of a hotel south of Berlin. The first gazing session took place in the morning at eight o'clock. After a brief explanatory introduction, we saw a clip from a DVD in which people spoke of the help they and their loved ones had received through Braco's gaze. Those of us present were advised to be entirely in the here and now with our thoughts and simply to wish the very best for us and our lives. Then Braco took the stage and his gaze shifted from one participant to the other. I had come to the meeting with no expectations. I could clearly feel that there was something special in this man's gaze. It's difficult to describe the wave of emotion that took hold of me when I looked Braco in the eyes. The experience is always very personal. As Braco looked at the participants from the podium in stillness, I recognized and felt a connection to something that had been barely noticeable to me before. Now it was present, and it grew stronger and stronger in the following years and established itself as part of a new phase of life. I can't find the words for what happened in me at that moment. A deep sense of joy took hold of me. I felt liberated and relieved. I was full of energy. With a wide smile on my face, I started the journey home. This inner joy would last for more than a week. A new attitude toward life had signaled its arrival.

My first encounter with Braco's gaze was followed by others—each with its own personal experience. Through what is conveyed by Braco, my life has been fundamentally transformed in a way I couldn't have imagined at the time. The change in where I lived and worked made everyday life more fulfilling for me. I found a work environment that incorporated my own self-actualization, including treasured colleagues and new friends (after years of stagnation). My life has become more intentional. I've found more energy to take care of upcoming tasks and organize my life. Minor health problems have simply rolled past—I'm doing better than I was years ago. Even if the calendar says something different—I feel younger, mentally more flexible and borne by deep confidence in a positive future. I'm convinced that Braco is able to convey something that can make people happier and improve their lives in many ways. That alone would make it worth setting out on this path. First came my personal experience, and then over time it was confirmed by very remarkable reports from people who had visited events in Europe or Braco's center in Zagreb.

Braco doesn't refer to himself as a healer, and he says that the power that people feel when they encounter his gaze doesn't come from him. Scientific explanations are still being sought. There are some promising approaches to explanations that are based in part on old and new findings in physics. Invisible connections in the cosmos, vibrations, information transfer, quantum physics like the unified field theory, for example—all these can offer starting points for explanatory models in which positively influencing the human organism independent of physical contact is as self-evident as the flow of electricity is for people in the twenty-first century.

Uwe-Michael Truhn, Psychologist and Psychotherapist, Germany

I met Braco in 2008. A friend had told me about him. After a conference, without my knowing much, we drove to the building at 1 Srebrnjak Street, Braco's center in Zagreb. As soon as I got out of the car, I felt something familiar and warm and a lot of energy. It was already evening, and we were standing in front of a locked door. The gate with the butterfly symbol was locked. Despite that, I was experiencing a great deal in my body and soul. And I knew inside me that this was something very special. All my doubts and skeptical feelings disappeared on the spot. A good friend told me that this place reminded her of the Garden of Gethsemane in Israel. I could understand what she meant quite well. There was something sacred and at the same time inexpressible about it. A year later, I saw Braco in person for the first time, first in the summer with his voice in Zagreb and then in Stuttgart with his giving gaze. I was there with my wife. After the first meeting, we were both in a special state. We felt a strong feeling of happiness and were lifted up inside. And this continued. We went to a crowded restaurant. I was sitting with my back directly to the aisle. Normally that would bother me a lot. Not this time. I only felt calm, peace and happiness in every cell of my body.

After that, I volunteered to help several times to keep the sessions running smoothly at large events. In Munich-Unterschleissheim, I was on site with several doctors as medical support staff. I myself am a psychologist and also have my own psychotherapy practice. So I was given the task of tending to people with psychovegetative disorders, fear or agitation. Sometimes after a session with Braco, people can experience extraordinary feelings or emotionally or psychologically atypical conditions. However, these feelings often settle within a short time after meeting with Braco. Something new, something previously unfamiliar or even unknown, has touched their soul. Much often happens without our understanding it, let alone consciously perceiving it. We come into contact with a clear mirror that looks at us and sees us, and in which we can feel and see ourselves more ("mirroring"). In this way, we learn to perceive our inner world better, to accept our desires and fears. Fundamental to this is the feeling of being looked at and seen as a whole person. We feel loved in its gaze—like a child feels loved by her parents. A well-known psychoanalyst speaks of children being reflected in the sparkle of their parents' eyes. Over the years, I've been able to observe myself and many other people as we have more and more become the people we really are, after previously not daring to accept ourselves and this nucleus in us. It makes us stronger and more resilient for the many and often difficult tasks in our daily lives. Over a longer period of encounters with Braco and his giving gaze, we regrow from the ground up. Everything in our lives, from flaws and false role models up to traumatic experiences we've had, becomes more and more filled with this loving energy. It becomes softer; we can't avoid weeping; it's as if it becomes liquefied. And what psychoanalysts call "libidinal cathexis" begins to grow in us. This means that this loving energy permeates our bodies and our entire being and remains more and more with us and in us. We feel more loved, consider ourselves more lovable, and are able to love other people more, which in turn has a positive effect on us. This process automatically leads to improved self-esteem and more stable protection for everything in everyday life that flows against us or seeks to penetrate us.

Personally, it helps me greatly in my work with my patients to always have the opportunity to recharge myself with the gaze or the voice of Braco and then be there again for my patients. It's just good to hear Braco's voice or to watch his gaze via live stream after a long day at the practice. After a few sessions I suddenly feel free again, even empty in a positive sense. Psychoanalysis speaks here of "negative capacity," a kind of empty space like a vacuum that is ready to take in everything that comes from the patient. The encounter with Braco has repeatedly helped me to clear myself mentally. Afterward, calmness of thought and a feeling of wellbeing and power set in. I'm very happy and grateful to know Braco and to know that I can profitably utilize him in my daily life for myself and for everyone I meet.

Matthias Knöringer, Medical Doctor, Specialist in Rehabilitative Medicine, Germany

I went to an event with Braco for the first time years ago because on the one hand I was looking to broaden my intellectual horizons, and on the other hand, as a doctor, I was interested in the way Braco helps people. I have to admit that after the first, highly anticipated meeting, I was a little disappointed with his gaze. Everything went very quickly. The encounter was introduced with just a few words. What I hadn't really paid attention to at first was this pleasant feeling in my chest, which persisted for days after the encounter. Today I know that this very specific energy, which many describe as a feeling of love, is the essential thing. Since then, I haven't wanted to be without a connection to this type of energy source again. At this point I've accompanied Braco to several events. The first thing I noticed is his modesty and tremendous authenticity. He's just himself. During the events, which often start early in the morning and end in the late afternoon, he waits between meetings in rooms behind the stage that are sometimes extremely sparse. He's often traveling for days on end from one meeting site to the next. Yet he's always in balance and full of energy. When I ask people what they felt while he gazed at them, the most common answer is: love. What is it that makes you feel love and brings tears to your eyes under the gaze of another human being? And where is the connection when people subsequently report improvements in their mental or physical conditions? For years I've had the opportunity to speak to many participants at events. With determination, people report back about positive changes in their lives and their new, unshakable faith and confidence in a positive future for themselves and their neighbors. You often hear, of course, that not all problems disappear, but that people now have the inner stability and strength to cope with all their challenges much more easily. How is it possible for years of chronic pain, depression, addictions and similar problems to sometimes simply disappear completely?

An elderly lady in Esslingen told me how she had become free of severe back pain. Previously, she was only able to walk a few meters with the help of a walker and eventually even needed nursing care. She showed me the medical findings, including MRI diagnostics, which described the presence of advanced stenosis of the lumbar spine—a bony constriction of the spinal canal that can actually only be treated surgically. An operation of this kind had been recommended to her. She reported:

> Then in February 2015 I saw Braco in Munich. Two of my friends had to prop me up under my arms so I could get into the session room. During the session I felt a strong current throughout my body and the pain was almost unbearable. Despite that, I believed that it could only mean something good. And in fact, when the session was over, I was able to walk normally again, with no pain and without any help whatsoever. My two friends who had helped me in were extremely surprised. It's remained like that to this day. I walk without a walker, I can get up without support, climb stairs, and so on.

For me, as a doctor who deals with these pathologies on a daily basis, there's no way to explain how there could be spontaneous freedom from pain after a bony constriction of the spinal canal. When people have experienced a healing like this, I've never heard of them looking for explanations of how it came about. I don't want to try to explain Braco's work, although there are quite a few convincing, scientifically sound explanatory approaches. But as a doctor I feel the need to say how important it is—especially in medicine—to recognize the true core of our being and to be open to possibilities that can profoundly help us. In science we often overlook the fact that when investigating phenomena that are new to us, we refer to previously existing explanatory models or theories. If we're investigating a phenomenon that is beneficial to people's health, for example, often it doesn't matter how impressive the results are. They're rejected because they don't fit into an existing explanatory framework, in keeping with the motto "That which is not allowed to exist must therefore be impossible." But for many scientists who are engaged in practice such as medical doctors, what counts are the results. If something helps a patient, they'll recommend it or use it, regardless of whether or not they can explain how it works. As a doctor in a specialist practice that accepts public health insurance, I experience people's afflictions every day. If you monitor a person over a longer period of time, you'll learn more about the background of the illness of the person in question. With young people, it's often anxious thoughts about the future. With adults, it's partly from past injuries to the soul, later sheer exhaustion from using up their vitality.

People who come to events with Braco have told me that when they encounter Braco they not only feel more physical energy, but also see the world from a more positive perspective, a perspective of abundance. What's particularly astonishing is that improvements also occur over the Internet, that is, without Braco being present in person. Especially in today's globalized world, live streaming is a perfect opportunity to reach people and help them. A woman who came to events in Zurich reported the following to me:

A year ago I was having severe pain in my right knee and edema in both legs. The doctor took an X-ray and diagnosed osteoarthritis. I was given medication for the pain, which brought me some relief. But as things progressed, the pain became stronger. I could barely sleep and I cried a lot. After learning about Braco, I took part in an encounter with his gaze via live streaming in summer 2014. I felt what seemed like a giant wave of violet light and had the sensation that it was flowing through me. It felt like a shower inside me. The entire right side of my body, down to my foot, became very hot. Then after three sessions in a row, I was so exhausted that I went to bed. I was able to sleep through the night for the first time in a month. When I woke up the following morning and was having coffee, I thought that something was different and suddenly realized that I was no longer in pain. The edema had also disappeared. I haven't needed pain pills since.

When people encounter Braco's gaze, they find calm. There's no information they have to think about. In this moment, Braco seems to be a projection screen for pure presence in which the participants immerse themselves while experiencing his gaze. It seems that in the process, some experience a higher plane of consciousness—a higher plane that's not disturbed by negativity, but where there's only love, a plane of unlimited possibilities. With Braco, there's no treatment of symptoms. As a doctor, it's also important for me to emphasize that seeing Braco isn't an alternative to medical treatment. Braco doesn't see himself as a healer. Braco won't eliminate problems, but he will awaken something in people that brings about change and helps them lead happy, self-directed lives.

Rudina Thanassi, Medical Doctor, Author and Specialist in Dermatology and Plastic Surgery, Albania

I've recommended Braco to many of my friends and patients who were experiencing difficulties and others who were doing well with their lives but showed interest. Most of them were very open toward Braco and had a good, peaceful feeling after experiencing his gaze.

I have seen remarkable improvements with health conditions and help with social, economic and emotional issues when people started to open up to Braco and his gaze. In my memory, some of these cases have had a big impact for years. The first time, I recommended Braco to a childhood friend. She had asked me for medical help. I was happy to help her with her skin conditions and recommended a new doctor for her back pain, for which she had been treated in Albania and Germany for more than ten years. One morning she started crying and told me that her skin and back conditions weren't the most serious problems she was facing in her life at the time. She was unable to work because her husband was schizophrenic and couldn't leave the house or even be alone with her. She couldn't even walk her young child to school. She was so desperate that she had contemplated killing herself and her child just to save them from a life of poverty, disease and suffering. None of the medical treatments or medications that her husband had received in Germany or Albania were able to improve his condition. So I told her about Braco. I told her that Braco wasn't a doctor, but since she had tried everything and had nothing to lose, she could try Braco and his gaze for herself. Well, in less than six months, her husband was functional again. He went back to work after 15 years, had friends again and has been getting out of the house ever since then. She got a job that was better than she had dreamed of in a very prominent and well-paid position with a wonderful environment and comfortable working hours. They're all happy and healthy and leading normal lives today. She now recommends Braco to everybody.

One of my patients asked me for help with her son. He was 17 years old and addicted to drugs. I told her to seek help from a specialist in toxicology and psychiatry, but she told me that she had already tried everything for years. Then I told her to experience Braco and his gaze. After some time she came to me again, very happy and radiant. Her son was doing well. He went back to school and earned outstanding grades, and she and her husband got back together and discovered that they loved each other.

Another case involved an old friend of mine I met again after six years. At first I didn't recognize her. Physically, mentally and emotionally, she was in poor shape. She was a highly educated woman, but for at least 18 months had had no work or income at all. She had numerous family problems, lots of debt, all kinds of problems, a compromised relationship and very low self-esteem. Many things had been out of place in her personal life for many years, and things were starting to get even worse. Her situation was so desperate that I didn't know how to help her. I recommended that she should watch encounters with Braco's gaze, since there was a live online broadcast that day. Since then, developments have gone step by step in the right direction: her health, her appearance, her self-esteem, her work, her emotional and mental health, her family situation, her relationships, her family business, her status. She paid off all her debts and also most of the family debts. Everything has changed for the best, and she even resolved problems that went back 20 years. She's a happy person now and her family is completely changed.

Aleksandar Racz, PhD, Professor at the University of Applied Health Sciences in Zagreb

We try to find an explanation of the Braco phenomenon in the roots of medicine, in old theories that allow not only for a description of the chemical processes of the visible and material body, but also for the existence of life forces and vital energies, which in the past have been called by various names...This life force is omnipresent, it is life itself, and it goes far beyond physical existence. People like Braco have a special gift, a special ability to collect, channel and direct this omnipresent life force to the people who need it.[157]

Mufti Ševko Effendi Omerbašić, Former President of the Mešihat of the Islamic Community in Croatia and Slovenia

In conversation, [Braco] comes across as very gentle, almost childlike in naivety. He rejects all external aspects of power. He carries something powerful within him. It is the essence of his existence. I had the opportunity to see this spontaneity in his relationships with people. It's overwhelming. What's so impressive in conversation with him is the naturalness he possesses, and how he just looks as if he doesn't know where his powers come from.[158]

Epilogue

I do not try to prepare. I simply am. There is no 'technique,' no 'secret' and no 'method.' On the contrary, there is an absence of all that. There is nothing in this world that we can describe that is not a product of our rational mind and, as such, a part of the material Universe. In other words, it is beyond the reach of the deepest layers of our consciousness.[158]
Braco in conversation with Drago Plečko

For many years, in addition to my profession as a physician, I have been interested in spirituality and consciousness research and have also meditated regularly. I know that there are certain people who are always there at special times in world history with a very responsible task.

Since these individuals usually appear very simple and inconspicuous and bring up something completely new for their time, they are often not understood at first. But you can recognize them by their special humility and love and their unique nature. Unfortunately, we humans are made in such a way that we always prefer to believe what we have built up in our lives as a concept of truth, and we are not readily accessible to something new.

Who Braco is, why he is here during these times and what he brings can be understood in the heart. Some people feel that his gaze brings a direct connection to the Source. Thereby, the silence and his gaze prepare the way. It is a chance for people in these times to regain genuine and complete inner freedom and independence, in union with their true self. As a gift.

Braco with Matthias Kamp, MD

The secret of Braco's gift, his silent gaze, is not a secret, but a door that is open for every human being. But it is only when you take the first step, and find the courage to open yourself up to something that your mind and intellect do not understand, that you begin to understand through experience.

As I have already mentioned several times within this book: in our times, it is a challenge to leave behind common patterns and the need to explain everything, and to dare to take the first step into something unknown and new which is only accessible through feeling. This book has provided many examples, in the hope that the reader will set out on his or her own journey to get to know something that our time has set aside in the light of its fascination with the possibilities of science and technology: the unknown greatness and depth of our own life. Braco's gaze opens up a simple path to the miracle in people. It is the silence and his gaze that can open the door to your own soul, pave the way, and help you get to know yourself again.

Braco does not need any commandments, teachings or rules: what remains is the silence and his gaze. Everything lies within, for those who know how to use it.

There is just one tiny point in your body that fears of this world cannot harm. This point in you is dormant. I always try to awaken it. If I succeed, you will go home happy and no longer feel any fear.[159]

What I do is neither great nor grand. It is simply what I have to do. What I was created for. Just as it is naturally given to the nightingale to sing beautifully or to the tulips to delight the hearts of observers with their majestic colors, it is my human nature to try to help.[160]

(Braco in conversation with Drago Plečko)

Notes

1. Filmclip: *Joy of Life*, YouTube: Braco official channel
2. Personal report by Mia, visitor at an event in Opatija, Croatia, DVD: *Wir sind alle eins*
3. Written report by Florian N., testimonials, what visitors say: www.braco.me
4. Short statements from visitors at events in Croatia, USA and Austria
5. Schneider, *Braco: Die faszinierende Welt von Mythos und Wissenschaft*, p. 15f
6. ibid., p. 29
7. Gruden, *Bracos Blick 2*, p. 10
8. Short statements from visitors at events in Germany, Croatia, Austria and Switzerland
9. Personal report, conversation at the event
10. Personal report, conversation at the event
11. Personal report, conversation at the event
12. Personal report, conversations at the events in Memmingen, Germany; Marchtrenk, Austria; Munich, Germany
13. Personal report, conversation at the event
14. Written report by Julio, testimonials, what visitors say, www.braco.me
15. Written report by Prof. Dr. D. Dulcan, testimonials, what experts say, www.braco.me
16. Personal report by Dr. Rudina Thanassi
17. Personal report by Fred, USA, film: *Golden Bridge*, YouTube: Braco official channel
18. Personal report by Rob, USA, DVD: *Joy of Life*
19. Written report by Lorette, testimonials, what visitors say, www.braco.me
20. Personal report, conversation at the event
21. Personal report, DVD: *Wir sind alle eins*

22. Personal report, conversation at the event
23. Personal report, conversation at the event
24. Personal report, conversation during a meeting in Zagreb
25. Personal report, conversation at the event
26. Personal report, www.braco.me
27. Personal report, filmclip: *Event Los Angeles*, USA, live streaming, 2020
28. Personal report, DVD: *Vom Funken zur Flamme*
29. Schneider, *Braco: Die faszinierende Welt von Mythos und Wissenschaft*, p. 45
30. Personal report, conversation at the event
31. Personal report, film: *A Personal Encounter*, YouTube: Braco official channel
32. Personal report, DVD: *Dein Schein*
33. Plečko, *Das Mysterium Braco 3*, p. 197
34. Personal report at the event
35. Personal report, conversation at the event
36. Personal report, conversation at the event
37. Personal report, conversation at the event
38. Personal report, filmclip: *Event Los Angeles*, USA, live streaming, 2020
39. Gruden, *Bracos Blick 1*, p. 157
40. Excerpts from reports by visitors at events in Germany, Austria and Switzerland
41. Gruden, *Bracos Blick 1*, p. 71
42. ibid., p. 29
43. Personal report, film: *Ocean of Presence 1*, YouTube: Braco official channel
44. Gruden, *Bracos Blick 1*, p. 30
45. Plečko, *Das Mysterium Braco 3*, p. 198
46. Short statements from visitors at various events in Germany and Austria
47. Plečko, *Das Mysterium Braco 3*, p. 117

48. Short statements from visitors at various events in Germany, Croatia and Switzerland

49. Personal report, film: *Ocean of Presence 1*, YouTube: Braco offical channel

50. Aïvanhov, *Der Weg der Stille*

51. Talks on Sri Ramana Maharshi, narrated by David Godmann, YouTube

52. See note 48

53. Gruden, *Bracos Blick 1*, p. 170

54. ibid., p. 165

55. Gruden, *Bracos Blick 2*, p. 161

56. Gruden, *Bracos Blick 1*, p. 20f

57. Gruden, *Bracos Blick 2*, p. 56

58. ibid., p. 55

59. Personal report, documentary: *The Power of Silence*, YouTube: Braco official channel

60. Gruden, *Bracos Blick 1*, p. 160

61. Gruden, *Bracos Blick 2*, p. 75

62. Plečko, *Das Mysterium Braco 3*, p. 52

63. Plečko, *Das Mysterium Braco 2*, p. 145

64. Drago Plečko in conversation with Angelika Whitecliff; Whitecliff, *21 Tage mit Braco*, p. 84

65. Whitney Houston, 'One Moment in Time', lyrics, Internet

66. Plečko, *Das Mysterium Braco 3*, p. 155

67. Plečko, *Das Mysterium Braco 1*, p. 7

68. Plečko, *Das Mysterium Braco 3*, p. 132

69. Plečko, *Das Mysterium Braco 1*, p. 66f

70. ibid., p. 75f

71. Personal report, film: *Invisible Hug*, YouTube: Braco official channel

72. Plečko, *Das Mysterium Braco 1*, p. 27

73. ibid., p. 8

74. Plečko, *Das Mysterium Braco 3*, p. 42

75. Filmclip: *20 Years with Braco*, YouTube: Braco official channel
76. Personal report, live streaming, 2019
77. Gruden, *Bracos Blick 1*, p. 5
78. Gruden, *Bracos Blick 2*, p. 180
79. Gruden, *Bracos Blick 1*, p. 157
80. Gruden, *Bracos Blick 2*, p. 117
81. Personal report by a visitor, film: *Braco The Gaze of Light*, YouTube: Braco official channel
82. Personal report, DVD: *Die Geschichte über Braco*
83. Gruden, *Bracos Blick 1*, p. 169
84. ibid., p. 46
85. Gruden, *Bracos Blick 2*, p. 51
86. Gruden, *Bracos Blick 1*, p. 46
87. Gruden, *Bracos Blick 2*, p. 137
88. ibid., p. 178
89. Gruden, *Bracos Blick 1*, p. 175
90. Personal reports, film: *Braco The Gaze of Light*, YouTube: Braco official channel
91. Recording of Braco's voice, DVD: *Vom Funken zur Flamme*
92. Short statements from visitors at various events in Germany, Croatia and Switzerland
93. ibid., Germany, Switzerland, Croatia
94. Plečko, *Das Mysterium Braco 2*, p. 55
95. Plečko, *Das Mysterium Braco 3*, p. 47
96. Gruden, *Bracos Blick 1*, p. 55
97. ibid., p. 43f
98. ibid., p. 77
99. ibid., p. 44
100. ibid., p. 10
101. From conversations with visitors to events in Germany and Croatia
102. Gruden, *Bracos Blick 1*, p. 94f
103. Gruden, *Bracos Blick 2*, p. 171

104. Documentary: *The Power of Silence*, YouTube: Braco official channel
105. Gruden, *Bracos Blick 2*, p. 69f
106. ibid., p. 116
107. Carl Jung, *The Red Book*, p. 232
108. Gruden, *Bracos Blick 2*, p. 62f
109. Personal report, DVD: *Aufbruch*
110. Wiesendanger, *Das große Buch vom geistigen Heilen, Fernheilen Band 2*
111. ibid.
112. Prof. Dr. (rer. nat.) C. Turtur, *Forschungen zur Raumenergie*, Internet
113. Obituary Alex Schneider, Baseler PSI Verein
114. ibid.
115. Personal report, film: *A Personal Encounter*, YouTube: Braco official channel
116. Schneider, *Braco: Die faszinierende Welt von Mythos und Wissenschaft*, p. 6
117. Conversation between Professor Schneider and Angelika Whitecliff, *21 Tage mit Braco*, p. 114ff
118. Schneider, *Braco: Die faszinierende Welt von Mythos und Wissenschaft*, p. 23f
119. ibid., p. 45
120. ibid., p. 48f
121. Plečko, *Das Mysterium Braco 3*, p. 27
122. Whitecliff, *21 Tage mit Braco*, p. 11
123. ibid., p. 28
124. ibid., p. 204
125. ibid., p. 291
126. Personal report, DVD: *Liebe ist meine endgültige Prophezeiung*
127. Whitecliff, *21 Tage mit Braco*, p. 155f
128. Personal report, DVD: *Liebe ist meine endgültige Prophezeiung*
129. Whitecliff, *21 Tage mit Braco*, p. 175

130. Personal reports after visiting Ivica Prokić, DVD: *Leben nach dem Leben*

131. Personal report after visiting Ivica Prokić, DVD: *Lasting Memories*

132. Prokić, *Wie ich Prophet wurde*, p. 155f

133. ibid., 161f

134. Personal statement by Ivica Prokić, DVD: *Leben nach dem Leben*

135. Braco, *Nach der großen Tragödie*, p. 17f

136. Whitecliff, *21 Tage mit Braco*, p. 170

137. Personal report, DVD: *Liebe ist meine endgültige Prophezeiung*

138. Plečko, *Das Mysterium Braco 3*, p. 66

139. ibid., p. 152

140. ibid., p. 34

141. Written report by Moldow, testimonials, experts and celebrities about Braco, www.braco.me

142. Personal report, DVD: *Liebe ist meine endgültige Prophezeiung*

143. Personal report, film: *Braco Evolution: The Age of Live Streaming*, YouTube: Braco official channel

144. Personal report, film: *Braco Evolution: The Age of Live Streaming*, YouTube: Braco official channel

145. Personal report, film: *The Gaze of Light: Journey to Hawaii*, YouTube: Braco official channel

146. ibid.

147. Visitors after an event with the voice of Braco in Zagreb, DVD: *Vom Funken zur Flamme*

148. Personal report, DVD: *Aufbruch*

149. Personal report, conversation in Zagreb

150. Plečko, *Das Mysterium Braco 2*, p. 106

151. Short statements from visitors at events in Germany, Austria and Croatia

152. Plečko, *Das Mysterium Braco 3*, p. 32f

153. Personal report, conversation at the event

154. Report by Karen about her mother, event in San Francisco, live streaming, 2020
155. Short statement by a visitor from Croatia
156. Schneider, *Braco: Die faszinierende Welt von Mythos und Wissenschaft*, p. 97f
157. Personal report, film: *A Dream Comes True*, YouTube: Braco official channel
158. Plečko, *Das Mysterium Braco 3*, p. 197
159. ibid., p. 54
160. ibid., p. 57f

Bibliography

Aïvanhov, Omraam Mikhaël, *Der Weg der Stille*, Dietlingen, 2017

Braco, J. G., *Nach der großen Tragödie*, Zagreb, 2007

Gruden, Prof. Dr. Vladimir, *Bracos Blick 1, 2*, Zagreb, 2016, 2017

Jung, Carl, *The Red Book: Liber Novus*, ed. Sonu Shamdasani

Plečko, Drago, *Das erste Buch der Genesung*, Zagreb, 2005

Plečko, Drago, *Das Mysterium Braco 1, 2, 3*, Zagreb, 2006, 2008, 2015

Prokić, Ivica, *Wie ich Prophet wurde*, Zagreb, 2012

Schneider, Prof. Alex, *Braco: Die faszinierende Welt von Mythos und Wissenschaft*, Zagreb, 2011

Whitecliff, Angelika, *21 Tage mit Braco*, Zagreb, 2009

Wiesendanger, Dr. Harald, *Das große Buch vom geistigen Heilen*, Band 2, Schönbrunn, 2004

O-BOOKS

SPIRITUALITY

O is a symbol of the world, of oneness and unity; this eye represents knowledge and insight. We publish titles on general spirituality and living a spiritual life. We aim to inform and help you on your own journey in this life.
If you have enjoyed this book, why not tell other readers by posting a review on your preferred book site?

Recent bestsellers from O-Books are:

Heart of Tantric Sex
Diana Richardson
Revealing Eastern secrets of deep love and intimacy to Western couples.
Paperback: 978-1-90381-637-0 ebook: 978-1-84694-637-0

Crystal Prescriptions
The A-Z guide to over 1,200 symptoms and their healing crystals
Judy Hall
The first in the popular series of eight books, this handy little guide is packed as tight as a pill-bottle with crystal remedies for ailments.
Paperback: 978-1-90504-740-6 ebook: 978-1-84694-629-5

Take Me To Truth
Undoing the Ego
Nouk Sanchez, Tomas Vieira
The best-selling step-by-step book on shedding the Ego, using the teachings of *A Course In Miracles*.
Paperback: 978-1-84694-050-7 ebook: 978-1-84694-654-7

The 7 Myths about Love...Actually!
The Journey from your HEAD to the HEART of your SOUL
Mike George
Smashes all the myths about LOVE.
Paperback: 978-1-84694-288-4 ebook: 978-1-84694-682-0

The Holy Spirit's Interpretation of the New Testament
A Course in Understanding and Acceptance
Regina Dawn Akers
Following on from the strength of *A Course In Miracles*, NTI teaches us how to experience the love and oneness of God.
Paperback: 978-1-84694-085-9 ebook: 978-1-78099-083-5

The Message of A Course In Miracles
A translation of the Text in plain language
Elizabeth A. Cronkhite
A translation of *A Course In Miracles* into plain, everyday language for anyone seeking inner peace. The companion volume, *Practicing A Course In Miracles*, offers practical lessons and mentoring.
Paperback: 978-1-84694-319-5 ebook: 978-1-84694-642-4

Your Simple Path
Find Happiness in every step
Ian Tucker
A guide to helping us reconnect with what is really important in our lives.
Paperback: 978-1-78279-349-6 ebook: 978-1-78279-348-9

365 Days of Wisdom
Daily Messages To Inspire You Through The Year
Dadi Janki
Daily messages which cool the mind, warm the heart and guide you along your journey.
Paperback: 978-1-84694-863-3 ebook: 978-1-84694-864-0

Body of Wisdom
Women's Spiritual Power and How it Serves
Hilary Hart
Bringing together the dreams and experiences of women across the world with today's most visionary spiritual teachers.
Paperback: 978-1-78099-696-7 ebook: 978-1-78099-695-0

Dying to Be Free
From Enforced Secrecy to Near Death to True Transformation
Hannah Robinson
After an unexpected accident and near-death experience, Hannah Robinson found herself radically transforming her life, while a remarkable new insight altered her relationship with her father, a practising Catholic priest.
Paperback: 978-1-78535-254-6 ebook: 978-1-78535-255-3

The Ecology of the Soul
A Manual of Peace, Power and Personal Growth for Real People
in the Real World
Aidan Walker
Balance your own inner Ecology of the Soul to regain your
natural state of peace, power and wellbeing.
Paperback: 978-1-78279-850-7 ebook: 978-1-78279-849-1

Not I, Not other than I
The Life and Teachings of Russel Williams
Steve Taylor, Russel Williams
The miraculous life and inspiring teachings of one of the World's
greatest living Sages.
Paperback: 978-1-78279-729-6 ebook: 978-1-78279-728-9

On the Other Side of Love
A woman's unconventional journey towards wisdom
Muriel Maufroy
When life has lost all meaning, what do you do?
Paperback: 978-1-78535-281-2 ebook: 978-1-78535-282-9

Practicing A Course In Miracles
A translation of the Workbook in plain language, with
mentor's notes
Elizabeth A. Cronkhite
The practical second and third volumes of The Plain-Language
A Course In Miracles.
Paperback: 978-1-84694-403-1 ebook: 978-1-78099-072-9

Quantum Bliss

The Quantum Mechanics of Happiness, Abundance, and Health
George S. Mentz

Quantum Bliss is the breakthrough summary of success and
spirituality secrets that customers have been waiting for.
Paperback: 978-1-78535-203-4 ebook: 978-1-78535-204-1

The Upside Down Mountain

Mags MacKean
A must-read for anyone weary of chasing success and happiness
– one woman's inspirational journey swapping the uphill slog for
the downhill slope.
Paperback: 978-1-78535-171-6 ebook: 978-1-78535-172-3

Your Personal Tuning Fork

The Endocrine System
Deborah Bates
Discover your body's health secret, the endocrine system, and
'twang' your way to sustainable health!
Paperback: 978-1-84694-503-8 ebook: 978-1-78099-697-4

Readers of ebooks can buy or view any of these bestsellers by
clicking on the live link in the title. Most titles are published
in paperback and as an ebook. Paperbacks are available in
traditional bookshops. Both print and ebook formats are
available online.
Find more titles and sign up to our readers' newsletter at
http://www.johnhuntpublishing.com/mind-body-spirit
Follow us on Facebook at https://www.facebook.com/OBooks/
and Twitter at https://twitter.com/obooks